To Avoid Isolation

TO AVOID ISOLATION:

An Ambassador's View of U.S./ Japanese Relations

by **Yoshio Okawara**

UNIVERSITY OF SOUTH CAROLINA PRESS

Library of Congress Cataloging-in-Publication Data

Okawara, Yoshio, 1919–
    [Koritsuka o sakeru tame ni. English]
    To avoid isolation : an ambassador's view of U.S./ : Japanese
relations / by Yoshio Okawara.
      p. cm.
    Translation of: Koritsuka o sakeru tame ni.
    ISBN 0-87249-646-5
    1. United States—Foreign economic relations—Japan. 2. Japan—
Foreign economic relations—United States. 3. United States—
Politics and government—1981–   4. United States—Relations—Japan.
5. Japan—Relations—United States. I. Title.
HF1456.5J302613   1989   89-16695
335.52073—dc20   CIP

Contents

Preface

My first sight of America came in July 1951, when I arrived in foggy San Francisco aboard the U.S. army transport ship *General Collins*. I was then one of 480 Japanese students in the GARIOA [Government Account for Relief in Occupied Areas] program.

After spending the night in a dormitory at Mills College (a women's college in Oakland), I traveled by train across the American continent to Chicago and on to Syracuse, New York, for a six-week orientation at Syracuse University. After this, from the end of August until I returned to Japan in June of the following year (1952), I studied at New York University.

Coming to the United States from my own devastated and war-torn land, where everyday life was a matter of finding enough food to survive, America was to me a totally different world. I was profoundly struck by her vast land, her natural wealth, the beauty of her streets, and the cheerfulness of her people. It was as though the frog in the country well of the old Japanese proverb had been suddenly plucked up and set down in the midst of a great and marvelous city.

During the Kennedy years, I studied for ten months as a fellow at Harvard University's International Affairs Center, and then served as economic affairs councilor under Ambassador Ryuji Takeuchi. During the Nixon administration I was posted to the Embassy in Washington as Deputy Chief of Mission under Ambassador Nobuhiko Ushiba. Through all that time, initial impressions of America that I had gained as a foreign student never dimmed. This was the golden age of America's overwhelming power and undisputed leadership in the postwar world.

Most recently, I was privileged to serve for five years in Washington as my government's Ambassador to the United States.

During that time, I was greatly impressed with the depth and maturity that had developed in Japan-U.S. relations in the thirty or so years since the end of the war.

America has changed over the years, of course; her people were wearied by the Vietnam War and the Watergate scandal, and her economy had been buffeted by the first and second oil shocks. And as Japan developed into a strong economic power, there were changes in the way Japanese looked at the United States, and in the way Americans looked at Japan.

But it is a mistake to suppose that, because of these changes in our perspectives, the America of a former glory has completely passed away. In the most fundamental sense, America continues to hold tenaciously to its Americanness. It is a nation of phenomenal and enduring depth of spirit.

It is said that American behavior is subject to radical swings. But it is no less true — and dare not be forgotten — that America has shown a remarkable ability to quickly recover from its wilder swings. When the land boils over with emotional rhetoric, reasonable and rational reflection quickly asserts itself to put on the brakes.

Japan-U.S. economic friction has been argued about for a long time, but American censure of Japan has recently taken on a new severity. Why is this happening? And what should Japan's approach be in developing relations with the United States, the nation which has played such a decisive role in Japanese affairs, at every major turn in the 120 years of Japanese history since the visit of Commodore Perry and his *black ships*? We cannot allow our attention to be dominated by current events. We must probe deeply into every issue, and define our positions only after serious, methodical reflection.

In late January 1985, having been given my orders to return to Japan, I was extremely busy saying my formal goodbyes and making other return preparations. In the midst of all this I received an urgent message from a journalist friend in Tokyo. The gist of the message was as follows.

> Japan-U.S. economic friction must not be allowed to get any worse. No country is as important to Japan as the United States. Despite this fact, many economic leaders in Japan are complacent, and make no effort to understand why Americans are now leveling such scathing criticism at Japan.

As soon as you return, I urge you to sound the alarm in Japan, to tell the Japanese people exactly what the problems are. I urge you to impress upon all concerned the necessity of taking real steps to avoid being internationally isolated.

I returned to Japan on March 19. After reporting to Prime Minister Nakasone, Foreign Minister Abe, and other high-ranking figures in the government, I spoke before the Kasumi Club (a club for journalists assigned to the Ministry of Foreign Affairs), detailing recent developments in Japan-U.S. relations. I followed this up with speeches at the World Economic Research Institute, the Japan Press Club, and the Foreign Press Club. I explained in these speeches what was causing the friction, why U.S. congressional invective against Japan had become so harsh, why holding to the present course would inevitably make Japan an international orphan, and what Japan could do to save the situation.

Since that time, I have been inundated with speaking requests from all over the country, and continue today to travel widely for that purpose. This reflects how seriously many people here now view the current state of Japan-U.S. relations, and how worried they are about the way those relations will develop in the future.

It was while this was going on that I was contacted by my friend and former Foreign Ministry colleague, Eiji Tokura, now the managing director of the publishing house Sekai no Ugoki-sha. Mr. Tokura urged me to write a book based on my experiences in Washington over the past five years. By writing such a book, he explained, I could inform my countrymen of the real situation, and delineate the course which Japan should now take as a powerful international nation.

I had never dreamed of writing a book, and hesitated to take such a step. After many strong urgings not to neglect my duty to the Japanese people, however, I agreed to do my best. This book is the result.

I wish that I could have organized my thoughts better and written some passages more lucidly. But I have sought to faithfully set forth the plain realities of current Japan-U.S. relations, and drawing upon my experiences as Ambassador to the United States, to enable the reader to better understand what is going on in America today. I will be deeply gratified should this book be read with profit by thinking people, in whatever walk of life. It is my hope that it will contribute in some small way to the task of guiding our nation safely through this time of contention and avoiding the tragedy of international isolation.

I wish to heartily thank Tokyo University Professor and veteran America scholar Nagayo Homma for so graciously consenting to interview me for this book. I also greatly appreciate the support given me in this endeavor by several offices in the Ministry of Foreign Affairs. A very special word of thanks is deserved by all those who worked with me at the Embassy in Washington, D.C., whose professional dedication and unstinting support I will never forget.

August 20, 1985
Yoshio Okawara

To Avoid Isolation

1

America Comes to Her Senses

I arrived in Washington as the new Japanese ambassador on April 2, 1980. At the time, the United States was in a state of agitation over the Iran hostage crisis. There had been talk of Japan importing Iranian oil, and many Americans were extremely critical of Japan, asking why we were aiding Iran, an enemy of the United States. Just a few months before this, in December 1979, then Secretary of State Cyrus Vance severely reproached Foreign Minister Saburo Okita, saying "Isn't Japan being rather too callous about this?" To me, having just taken my post, this problem over importing Iranian oil was most distressing. One of America's three major television networks asked me to appear on their morning talk show. Unfortunately I had not yet formally presented my credentials, and so, after much agonizing over the decision, I declined the request.

As it turned out, Japan decided not to import Iranian oil, believing that the price was too high. But whatever the reason, once it was understood that Japan had decided not to import oil from Iran, the American mood changed dramatically. It was mid-April. The *New York Times* ran an editorial entitled "Thanks, and Oil to Japan," and eventually the voices of censure against Japan fell silent. This experience early in my posting to Washington, of American public opinion volatile one moment and subdued the next, made a tremendous impression on me.

My ambassadorial credentials were soon presented to President Jimmy Carter. Mr. Carter had been elected in 1976 in the aftermath of the Watergate scandal by an America anxious to heal the wounds left from the Vietnam War, but the second oil crisis had thrown the U.S. economy into recession; inflation was rampant and the prime rate was over 20 percent. As the economy sagged, the unemployment rate climbed steadily higher. Internationally, the United States was being humiliated by the hostage-holding Iranians. There was a general loss of confidence among Americans everywhere.

Then, in late 1979, the Soviet Union launched an armed invasion against Afghanistan. International public opinion was turned decisively against the Soviets. An extremely critical problem for the United States (against the backdrop of this solidification in world opinion) became the question of what sort of policies it should employ against the Soviet Union. The issue demanding an immediate decision was whether or not to participate in the 1980 Summer Olympics that were to be held in Moscow. The Carter administration imposed sanctions against the Soviet Union and advocated a boycott of the Moscow games. The American Olympic Committee subsequently agreed with this policy. In the International Olympic Committee, however, and in the various national Olympic committees, there was a strong desire to keep politics from interfering in sporting activities. This meant that it would not be easy for the Carter administration to get the rest of the free world to join its boycott. In Japan too the question of what stance should be taken was debated openly and vigorously. Out of consideration for Japan-U.S. relations and Western solidarity, the government was obliged to urge both the Japan Amateur Sports Association and the Japan Olympic Committee to decide not to participate, while being prepared to accept whatever decision these bodies finally reached. In the end, Japan and the other major free-world nations did boycott the Moscow Olympics. With the Iran hostage crisis still unresolved, however, the mood in America did not change for the better.

In the November elections of 1980, despite the advantages of incumbency, President Carter lost to Ronald Reagan, the Republican candidate. This reflected, I believe, the desire of the American people to restore their waning self-confidence and start anew with a fresh agenda.

The Reagan administration took over the reins of government in early 1981 and began implementing policies that were collectively referred to by critics as "Reaganomics." The U.S. economy began recovering, and by the end of Reagan's first term inflation had been brought under control, the rise in the consumer price index had settled down to around 4 percent, and interest rates had dropped, with the official discount rate down to 8 percent and the prime rate in the neighborhood of 10.5 percent. Unemployment — which had reached double-digit proportions — backed off to around 7.3 percent. America was transformed.

In the area of foreign relations, President Reagan's basic policy was to pursue talks with the Soviet Union from a position of strength, while making progress in arms control negotiations in the interest of world peace. A concerted effort would be made to bolster the nation's military capabilities, which had been neglected during the 1970s. Steps would also be taken to strengthen ties in the Western alliance. This was to be the background against which negotiations with the Soviets would be conducted.

In retrospect, the road over which the administration would have to travel in order to restructure East-West relationships according to the Reagan blueprint was by no means an easy one. To begin with, it was no simple task to achieve a consensus among the nations of the Western alliance. An example of America's difficulties can be seen in the Falkland Islands conflict that broke out in the spring of 1982. The United States was torn between its traditional ties with Britain and its position vis-à-vis Argentina, the latter being a key element in the administration's diplomatic agenda in Central and South America. Secretary of State Alexander Haig, Jr., undertook a vigorous shuttle-diplomacy effort to achieve conciliation between the two combatants, but this only succeeded in provoking anti-American sentiment among the British. This dilemma was followed by another in the fall when disagreement over laying the Soviet pipeline developed between the alliance members in Western Europe and the United States. The Western Europeans angrily charged the United States with forcing its will down their throats in addition to always thinking only of its own priorities and disregarding Western European economic interests. The Americans stressed their concern for NATO security, should the Western Europeans be exploited by the Soviet Union in their pursuit of economic gain. Japanese support was sought by both sides, forcing Japan — which had been deepening its economic ties with the Soviet Union — to face a difficult dilemma. But the Japanese government strove to achieve mutual conciliation in the interest of strengthening free-world solidarity, and in the end a breach between the United States and the other Western nations was averted. These experiences had a direct bearing on later efforts to achieve unity in the Western alliance to resolve disputes about the deployment of the Pershing II and cruise missiles.

Prime Minister Yasuhiro Nakasone had an active hand in drafting the declaration of Western solidarity issued at the Williamsburg Summit in 1983, which was interpreted by the United States and the European Community as an unequivocal statement of Japan's intention to play a political role as a full member of the Western alliance. This made a particularly strong impact in America, where it was seen as an indication of Japan's readiness to further broaden and deepen its relations with the United States.

In the U.S.-Soviet Intermediate Nuclear Forces (INF) and Strategic Arms Reduction Talks (START) negotiations being conducted at this time in Geneva, the Soviet Union adopted a diplomatic approach that sought to exploit any internal rift among the Western powers. However, the United States, by demonstrating that it could carry through with the existing policy of deploying the Pershing IIs and surface-launched cruise missiles in Western Europe (supported mainly by Britain and West Germany), was able to engage in these negotiations from a position of strength.

Meanwhile, acutely aware of the strategic threat imposed against Japan and other northeast Asian nations by the deployment of Soviet SS-20 missiles in Siberia, Japan strongly urged the United States to negotiate with the Soviets in the INF talks from a truly global perspective, not one biased toward Europe. The Americans fully recognized the Japanese position and thereafter negotiated with the Soviets from a global perspective rather than focusing solely on Europe. This also contributed to Western solidarity.

On September 1, 1983, the Korean Air jetliner was shot down. In the ensuing direct confrontation between the United States and the Soviet Union, Japan cooperated with the United States as an allied nation providing support that was greatly appreciated by the American people.

Americans are a very patriotic people, as evidenced by the ever-present "Stars and Stripes," which is flown from every public building. American patriotism reached a peak during the 1984 Summer Olympics in Los Angeles. The Soviet Union and Eastern-bloc nations (Rumania excepted) boycotted the games in retribution for the West's boycott of the Moscow Olympics. The absence of the Soviet athletes, however, resulted in the American team winning an enormous number of gold, silver, and bronze medals, victories that stirred up American patriotism all the more. Millions all across the land watched on television as American athletes stood proudly on the victory stand, and in one unforgettable scene people were shown enthusiastically waving American flags on the television screen.

Similarly, at both the Democratic convention held in San Francisco in July 1984, and the Republican convention held the following month in Dallas, the convention halls were filled with delegates waving little flags. When the Democrats nominated Walter Mondale, and again when the GOP nominated Ronald Reagan, the nominees looked out over wave upon wave of fluttering flags held high above faces that beamed with pride and satisfaction. This high degree of patriotism had not been seen four years earlier at the Democratic convention in Detroit or the Republican convention in New York.

In the early 1980s, to change the subject slightly, there was a boom in books and seminars on Japanese management methods. Ezra Vogel's *Japan as Number One* was one example, which in translation became a bestseller in Japan, but it did not sell too well in the United States, where extravagant praise of Japan does not seem to go down well. Nonetheless, for some while Japanese managerial techniques were enthusiastically discussed in various quarters. To try to explain this, I think there was a period when American managers were unsure of their methods, during that time when the United States was experiencing a general loss of self-confidence and the economy was in decline. It was in that psychological context that interest naturally turned to the methods being used so successfully by Japanese managers. During this same period the *Book of Five Rings* attributed to Miyamoto Musashi (a Japanese warrior) created a boomlet of its own, and a powerful figure in the Carter administration said to me, "You know, the reason American companies have to look to Japanese management techniques now goes right back to weaknesses in the management techniques taught at Harvard Business School." (The person who said that was not a Harvard graduate, by the way, and may have been suffering an attack of the "Harvard complex.")

5

These doubts concerning American business practices gradually subsided as the U.S. economy recovered, and nobody mentioned the *Book of Five Rings* any more. This suggested to me that American managers had regained their confidence both in the American economy and in their own managerial methods. It was after this recovery that one began to hear people saying, "the Japanese have become too arrogant." The following joke made the rounds of the Washington cocktail parties:

An American, a Frenchman, and a Japanese were abducted by Arab terrorists. "We are going to shoot you in five minutes," announced the terrorists to their captives, "Do you have any last words?"

"Allow me to sing my national anthem," said the Frenchman, and gave a throaty rendition of the Marseillaise.

Then the Japanese stepped forward and said, "Let me say just a few words about Japanese managerial techniques."

Hearing this, the American jumped up and shouted, "If we're going to have to listen to any more about Japanese managerial techniques, shoot me first!"

What was going on here? Well, now that their products were selling so well on the American market, the Japanese (taking great pride in their business expertise) had begun to think they had no more to learn from America, and that the time had come to teach America a thing or two. At least that seems to be the view taken by some informed Americans and by those having business dealings with the Japanese. Part of the exasperation exhibited by American industrialists seems to involve an intolerance for this perceived "Japanese arrogance."

Another experience comes to mind in this connection. Each year the Japanese Embassy sponsors a joint conference on trade in the United States which is attended by key Embassy officials, Consuls General, and representatives of Japanese corporations. The 1980 conference was held in Chicago. This was during the period of lapsed American self-confidence when much was being said about Japanese arrogance. Some of the conferees of the younger generation voiced the opinion that America's economy was seriously ill (in view of the technical level of her work force, the attitude toward work, and the productivity of her industry) and that America's future was bleak.

This opinion was opposed, however, by an older group of

presidents of Japanese-American companies based in New York. "We think that this pronouncement of the demise of America based on single-facet perceptions of surface phenomena is rather too shallow and haughty," they argued. "This country today is indeed dispirited and tormented by self-doubt. But what we need to focus on and understand now is rather America's latent power, and its ability to recover." And so the question of whether a failing America could be resuscitated was vigorously debated.

Particularly memorable was an elderly conferee who stated his opinion in the following words. "In addressing these issues, we need to do so with a modesty which recognizes that Japanese industry is being allowed to do business here in one small corner of the American marketplace." Coming as it did from a member of the "elders" who had already lived and worked for so many years in the United States, this statement carried a lot of weight.

Looking now upon the subsequent recovery of the U.S. economy and the concomitant restoration of American self-confidence, I think that the fundamental truth of that elder conferee's perception has been amply demonstrated.

It has often been pointed out that, in the course of events which led to the outbreak of World War II, our leaders in the government misjudged the power of the United States and thus led us down the tragic road to war. We must never again be beguiled by the merely phenomenal and underestimate America's true power.

Through the process of economic recovery, the American people regained the self-confidence needed to restore U.S. prestige in international politics. President Reagan was able to claim in his State of the Union message to Congress in 1984 that "America is back in shape, and there's good reason to believe that improvement will continue through the days to come." He went a step further in the 1985 message to Congress, declaring that the "time has come to proceed toward a great new challenge — a second American revolution of hope and opportunity."

In the national election in November 1984, President Reagan carried 49 states (losing only Minnesota and the District of Columbia) in his overwhelming reelection victory. This surely is a reflection of the restoration of American self-confidence and pride.

Returning to the subject of the Vietnam War and its after-effects, April 30, 1985, marked the tenth anniversary of the fall of Saigon. The Vietnam War is a painful subject for Americans, one which they would just as soon forget. Now the Vietnam Veterans Memorial has been built in black stone not far from the Lincoln Memorial in Washington, D.C., and the soldiers who fought in that war can now walk with pride through the city. This has even been reported in the media as the "rehabilitation of the Vietnam War" to a place of legitimacy.

At the same time, there is a strong feeling among Americans that they must never repeat the tragedy of the Vietnam War, which left such bitter memories. That is why both the presidential administration and Congress are compelled to approach the problems in Central America delicately and circumspectly. They know that the situation in Nicaragua must never be allowed to escalate into another Vietnam War.

In October 1983, the United States sent an expeditionary military force into Grenada which achieved its major objectives in a matter of hours. This overwhelming success gave a great psychological boost to Americans in helping to restore national self-confidence.

In sociological terms, I believe there is evidence of a major shift in awareness among the younger generation in America. The gradual trend among affluent American young people toward moderately conservative views — with the formerly overwhelming tendency to support the Democratic Party now shifting toward support for the Republican Party, or at least toward parity — is now a major aspect of America's social evolution. The movement that led to Ronald Reagan's victory in the 1980 elections has been characterized as a resurgence of conservatism among Americans. I think that the outcome of the 1984 elections, however, was not merely a reconfirmation of this conservative resurgence, but also the result of the spread of moderately conservative viewpoints among a broader segment of the population.

2

Japanese-American Economic Friction

The recent phenomenon of Japanese-American "economic friction" or "trade friction" is occurring despite the current recovery of the U.S. economy. This peculiarity is something that I think we must carefully examine.

In 1980 and 1981, from the closing days of the Carter administration and into the early period of the Reagan administration, the U.S. economy was at the bottom of a recession, unable to extricate itself from the ravages of the second oil shock. The consumer price index was climbing at 13.5 percent annually, bank lending rates were up over 20 percent, the Federal Reserve discount rate reached as high as 14 percent, and for a time the unemployment rate was in double-digit figures. It was in this context that the Reagan administration began to implement the supply-side economic policy of "Reaganomics." These policies included income tax cuts (reducing the maximum rate from 75 percent to 50 percent) and other tax cuts (implemented through an accelerated depreciation schedule) designed to promote greater investment incentives. The main objective of these policies was to reactivate the U.S. economy by stimulating private-sector activity. The three economic policy pillars were "small government," "deregulation," and "lower taxes." At first these policies did not seem to be all that effective, and many outspoken dissenters cautioned the nation not to expect much.

But in mid-1982 the U.S. economy began to recover. The inflation rate, bank lending rates, and unemployment rate all began to drop, and people began to extol the virtues of Reaganomics, as America advanced beyond other industrialized nations in terms of the pace of its economic recovery. This led to sharply increased imports to feed surging consumer demand, which in turn exacerbated the trade imbalance. America's trade deficit with Japan grew to $19.0 billion in 1982, $21.7 billion in 1983, and $36.8 billion in 1984 (Department of Commerce statistics; FAS basis for exports, CIF basis for imports).

To be sure, the proportion of the U.S. trade deficit attributable to Japanese trade was declining from 1982 to 1984, from roughly half in 1982 to about a third in 1983 and to less than 30 percent in 1984. This is indicative of how large the trade deficit was becoming (totaling $123.3 billion in 1984), with U.S. trade going into the red with more and more countries. No matter how far the proportion attributable to Japan declines, however, in American eyes no other country is amassing such enormous trade surpluses. Japan is the problem, then, and the focus of American attack. The United States has gradually lost its competitive edge in such industries as steel, automobiles, and machine tools — fields traditionally considered the industrial backbone of the nation — and there is now undeniably a sense of injury and crisis, a feeling that this trend will be disastrous for U.S. industry if not checked.

In his best-selling autobiography *Iacocca,* Lee Iacocca, the chairman of Chrysler Corporation, warns of the "Japanese challenge" at every turn. Here are some excerpts [from Japanese translation]:

"The United States is once again engaged in a great war with Japan. It doesn't seem so serious because thankfully it isn't the kind of war in which people die, but it is a war nevertheless, and we are heading straight into the jaws of defeat because our government fails to understand the true nature of the conflict."

"The economic war with Japan will determine America's future. Our adversary is a most formidable one. . . . Battlefields are typically marked by very uneven terrain, and this battlefield gives an enormous advantage to Japan."

"If we don't take action quickly, Japan will probably swallow up both the steel and automobile industries by the year 2000."

Iacocca's vehement language calls to an America that is charged with a crisis mentality, namely that it is headed for bitter defeat in the trade war with Japan if things go on as they are. It is a call to America to bestir itself. I don't believe that Iacocca is

10

narrow-mindedly anti-Japanese, but his book seems to accurately reflect both the pride and the exasperation of the U.S. automobile industry.

A similar state of mind is reflected in Motorola's Japanese-censuring media campaign in which it has repeatedly run prominent opinion ads in national weekly magazines and daily newspapers under the banner "How To Meet the Japanese Challenge."

The initial ads focused on how "unfair" Japanese competition is, but apparently some Americans opposed the content of these ads as altogether too scathing. Motorola then softened the tone of the ads and focused on how they were improving productivity in the face of Japanese competition and successfully turning out superior products. I don't believe there was any change in the underlying crisis mentality, however, and this campaign provides a relevant example of how U.S. industries are responding at the gut level to the pressure of Japanese competition.

To be sure, this crisis mentality did not suddenly appear when Ronald Reagan took office. Since the 1970s there had been much concern over how to cope with foreign competition in such fields as textiles, color TV's, electrical products, steel, and eventually automobiles. Hence one can see how enduring and pervasive this Japan-censuring mentality is.

In response to the sharp increases in the volume of Japanese goods coming into the American market, the affected U.S. companies adopted the policy of appealing for maximal assistance under existing legislation. In addition to petitions for the implementation of import remedy measures under Article 201 of the 1974 Trade Act, these companies filed numerous suits, making accusations of unfair trade practices under Article 301 of the same act, and invoking anti-dumping and antitrust laws. A classic example of this reaction was the Houdaille suit in 1982 and 1983 which involved exports of machine tools to the United States.

At the time, the U.S. market was being flooded with imported machine tools employing numerical control and other advanced technologies, and this was causing great alarm among U.S. manufacturers of machine tools. One of these manufacturers, Houdaille, charged that Japanese machine-tool manufacturers were being subsidized by government agencies, giving them an unfair competitive advantage, and filed a complaint with the International Trade Commission (ITC) that this constituted unfair competition under Article 301 of the Trade Act. The ITC took this case through the necessary procedures in the United States and rendered a decision of "guilty." The investigation conducted by the Department of Commerce pursuant to that decision and a subsequent study done by the White House both reached the same conclusion, namely that "remedy measures should be implemented in the face of the unfair competition from Japanese goods," which was made public under the authority of President Reagan. It was reported in the press, however, that the president killed this suit, having judged the proposed measures to be undesirable for Japan-U.S. relations.

There are many examples of such "guilty" decisions being handed down by the International Trade Commission, but there have also been quite a number of cases that ended in "innocent" verdicts, as in the case involving Japanese automobile exports to the United States. This has deepened the irritation felt in the industries involved, and as a result, the provisions for remedy and assistance under existing legislation came to be viewed as inadequate, and a movement to obtain new legislation or revise existing legislation gathered force. An extreme example of this is the so-called local content bill which was championed by the United Auto Workers (UAW) union as a way to cope with the automobile imports from Japan. This bill was pushed through Congress in 1982 and 1983 with the support of both Ford and Chrysler. It was passed by the House of Representatives in 1983, but died in the Senate without being debated.

A reciprocity bill has also been supported in Congress. In cases where a country that exports products to America failed to open its own markets to American goods, this bill would give the executive branch the right to impose collateral import restrictions. The philosophy embodied in the language of the original bill, however, was inconsistent with GATT (General Agreement on Tariffs and Trade) provisions, and on this basis the administration insisted that various conditions be attached. Eventually the bill was revised, with some of these conditions worked into the language, but the bill had a rough passage through Congress.

There was another vein of accusation coming from American industry at the time, charging that Japan was deliberately manipulating the market to achieve a weak yen and thereby inhibit U.S.

exports. With the prevailing strong dollar, and conscious of the great disadvantage to which this foreign-exchange situation put U.S. industry in confronting foreign competition, this argument sought to belabor Japanese industry (which enjoyed the advantage of a weak yen). In the face of this argument, the Treasury Department, the president's Council of Economic Advisors (CEA), and the Congressional Budget Office all conducted detailed studies from their respective points of view, and all reached the conclusion that there was absolutely no basis for the allegation that Japan had engaged in such currency manipulations. When these conclusions were made public, those voicing this argument were obliged to tone down their rhetoric. This did not, however, alleviate a real problem faced by U.S. businesses. No matter how diligently they work to improve their productivity, their hard-won increases can be completely nullified by a ten percent or 20 percent fluctuation in the exchange rate. Understandably these businesses desire a system in which exchange rates do not influence industrial competitiveness.

The problems of regulating international currencies have been the subject of unceasing international debate since the Venice Summit of 1980, but various nations have taken a negative stance toward radically revising the floating rate system that has been in effect since the Smithsonian accords were implemented in 1972. As a consequence, U.S. companies have abandoned any hope that the exchange rates can be regulated by currency policy, and have looked instead to the imposition of import surcharges. This is a mechanism that is advocated with particular forcefulness by the Business Roundtable, a powerful American business group. After concluding a series of meetings with the administration and Congress during his visit to the United States in January 1983, Prime Minister Nakasone invited a number of prominent figures in the U.S. business world to the Japanese Ambassador's residence for talks. Business Roundtable Chairman Lee Morgan (chairman of Caterpillar) and others present vigorously argued the necessity of correcting the weak-yen situation. Import surcharge mechanisms continued to be advocated, but past experience suggests that such mechanisms rarely achieve their objectives, and they have yet to elicit the support needed for implementation.

Some would argue that Japanese capital exports to the United States—seen as a major cause of the strong dollar and weak yen — should be restricted. According to the underlying analysis, the yen-denominated surplus that grows out of Japan's high savings rate is not expended in domestic consumption or channeled into domestic investments, but rather is invested in enormous quantities into the U.S. securities market thus causing the yen to weaken. The upshot of this analysis is that the flow of yen capital into the U.S. financial market should be restricted. This argument was pushed forward by C. Fred Bergsten, president of the Institute for International Economics and former assistant secretary in the Treasury Department during the Carter administration, but has failed to generate wide support.

Japanese industries have adopted various policies in response to this criticism by U.S. industry. Japan's steelmakers, for example, not only implemented self-imposed restrictions on exports to America in the 1970s, but also cooperated fully by submitting production cost reports in the late 1970s and early 1980s (when the United States introduced the so-called trigger-price mechanism which was keyed on Japanese steel production). This cooperation was greatly appreciated by the government in Washington. The Japanese steel industry also participated in the rehabilitation of the U.S. steel industry — which had fallen on bad times and was far behind in plant modernization — by sharing energy-saving technology and other technological advances. It was against this background that Japanese-U.S. negotiations became strained in connection with the Reagan administration's decision in September 1984, to implement what was in fact a quota system on steel imports, at the level of 18.5 percent. At the time, moreover, the imports of steel into the United States from Brazil, the Republic of Korea, and other emerging steelmaking nations were growing rapidly. The Japanese negotiators objected vigorously to this policy, as their steel industry was going to lose market share, and hence become an unwilling victim of the new quota system, precisely because of its cooperation with the United States. This was a pill too bitter to swallow. The negotiations bogged down, but the American negotiators refused to yield, insisting that President Reagan could not fudge on his public commitment. General agreement was finally reached in December at a quota level of 5.8 percent.

We come next to the problem of voluntary restrictions on automobiles. It was back in the mid-1960s, during my first tour of duty at our embassy in Washington, that Japan began exporting automobiles to the United States. I heard the stories going around at the time, that some make or other of Japanese car didn't have enough horsepower to climb the steep hills in San Francisco, that the cars couldn't do 60 mph on the expressways, that they shook violently when one tried to accelerate too fast, and so on. I well remember what one American Volkswagen dealer said at the time. "Japanese cameras are very highly regarded in America. Now if the Japanese can produce such excellent cameras, then make no mistake about it, soon they shall build cars that will be highly regarded here. I believe that day is coming." I'm not sure whether this was said by way of encouragement or sympathy. But sure enough, export to the U.S. market gradually expanded in the 1970s, and when the second oil shock hit in 1979, Japanese automobiles suddenly found themselves in the spotlight. A gasoline shortage developed, and a rationing system had to be implemented. Long lines of cars formed at gas stations. More and more American consumers turned from the large U.S.-made "gas hogs" to the smaller fuel-saving Japanese autos, a natural response under the circumstances. Against this background, Japanese auto exports to the United States grew very rapidly, with the market share jumping from 14.5 percent in 1979 to more than 20 percent in 1980. At that time the U.S. economy was still in deep recession, reeling from the impact of the second oil shock. Despite the rapid shrinkage of the U.S. automobile market, sales of Japanese cars were growing, creating a severe crisis mentality in Detroit, the center of American automobile production. Layoff figures rose to new highs with each passing month, reaching a maximum of 29 percent. Chrysler, one of the big three U.S. automobile manufacturers, was brought to the brink of bankruptcy and was only able to recover after a $1.5 billion congressional bailout. The encroachment of Japanese automobiles into the marketplace was very intimidating to U.S. automakers, and bills were introduced in Congress with the aim of restricting Japanese imports. When the Reagan administration took over in 1981, it was obliged to deal with this problem immediately, and from a very unenviable position. Having won on

15

a platform that championed anti-protectionism and free trade, the administration could hardly implement out-and-out import restrictions, but neither could it turn its back on the fate of the U.S. automakers and their workers. Faced with this dilemma, America resorted to the method that had been used before in resolving its trade problems with Japan — the appeal to Japan to implement voluntary restrictions.

The Reagan administration was in no position to serve Japan with an official request to take such action, and could only announce that the United States hoped that, in view of the situation in the U.S. auto industry and automobile market, Japan would take appropriate measures. Meanwhile, the Japanese were aware that the rapid increase in exports of cars to the United States was becoming a serious source of additional Japan-U.S. trade friction, and recognized the need for adopting a policy of "moderate and reasonable exports." This in turn presented the Japanese government with the problem of how to apportion these self-imposed restrictions among its own automakers. It would involve determining some specific numerical export quantities, while at the same time anticipating how such a policy would be affected by U.S. antitrust laws (which had been a perennial problem in trading with America).

A period of "quiet contact" ensued between Japan and the United States during which ways of resolving these problems were considered. On the one hand it was thought that high-level decisions should await the visit to Japan of Mr. William Brock, America's trade representative, who was immediately responsible for negotiating with Japan. However, Mr. Brock took an extremely equivocal position, holding that the Japan visit would be meaningless without achieving clear progress beforehand. At the end of March I returned to Japan briefly for consultations concerning the prime minister's visit to the United States. I discussed the American situation with the prime minister and certain members of his cabinet and urged them to adopt a prudent course. I also met privately with leaders in the Japanese automobile industry and exchanged opinions with them. As a result, nearly unanimous tacit agreement was reached on the "moderate and reasonable exports" approach. I then made a direct appeal to Brock to go ahead with the Japan visit.

Fortunately, when Mr. Brock went to Japan, the Japanese

16

negotiators had begun to recognize the difficulties that were confronting the U.S. auto industry and expressed a willingness to give the United States breathing time to overcome those difficulties. Specifically, the Japanese decision was to "limit auto exports to 1.65 million units a year for two years, then, from the third year on, deliberate future policy based on the results of the first two years." The implementation of self-imposed restrictions on auto exports to the United States was warmly applauded by the U.S. government.

The United Auto Workers and sympathetic members of Congress denounced the 1.65 million figure as entirely too large, but in view of subsequent developments, I think the voluntary restraint policy proved to be very significant for Japan-U.S. trade relations. Not only did the American automobile market recover, in the broader context of general U.S. economic recovery, but the U.S. auto industry made a remarkable comeback, and the number of workers either unemployed or laid off gradually came down.

When the third year rolled around, the Japanese decided to continue the 1.65 million unit restriction. With this the three-year restriction policy ended, but after weighing the American mood, Japan imposed a limitation of 1.85 million units in the fourth year, for one year only. In the spring of 1984, however, the Japan-U.S. trade imbalance again became disproportionately high and America was increasingly concerned about the posture Japan would adopt toward export limitations once the self-imposed restrictions ended in March 1985. While traveling around the United States to fulfill speaking engagements, I was almost always asked about this by the local media. In the meantime, however, consumer demand for automobiles had risen even higher, pulled along by continuing improvement in the U.S. economy, and automobile sales climbed to 11 million units in 1984. The comeback of the U.S. auto industry was truly remarkable, with top managers in the big three getting enormous bonuses that would be unthinkable in Japan. The Chrysler Corporation was able to pay back its $1.2 billion debt to the government at a single stroke.

Buoyed by these developments, Trade Representative Brock was able to say in the fall of 1984, "I personally think we no longer have any grounds for asking Japan for self-imposed restrictions on auto imports to the United States." The Reagan administration concurred, indicating that "the future is a clean slate." Soon after Reagan began his second term in office the President and his entire cabinet unanimously endorsed a position paper that spelled out the new policy that the United States would not ask Japan to continue its self-imposed restrictions after April 1985.

On March 28, 1985, the Ministry of International Trade and Industry (MITI) announced its decision to limit auto exports to the United States to 2.35 million units for one additional year beginning April 1. This decision gave consideration to the Japan-U.S. trade imbalance, to U.S. consumer demand, and to Japan automobile production being commissioned by General Motors and Chrysler for their sales. Despite the good intentions of the Japanese, however, this decision was roundly criticized in the United States, for a variety of reasons.

The 1970s had witnessed the Tokyo Round of tariff-reduction talks, which were promoted by Japan, at which the biggest problem on the agenda concerned agricultural products. Japan was ably represented in these talks by a formidable pair of tough and like-minded negotiators, namely the late Ichiro Nakagawa, who was the Minister of Agriculture, Forestry and Fisheries, and the late Nobuhiko Ushiba, serving as Minister of State for External Economic Affairs. These negotiations ended in the compromise now known as the Strauss-Ushiba agreement, which stated that "the import guidelines for such agricultural products as beef and oranges will be expanded in phases, culminating in 1983." Mr. Robert Strauss, the U.S. Special Trade Representative at the time, made a strong impression on the Japanese with his assertive Texas style, but the Americans for their part seemed to be even more astonished at the extremely strong negotiating style of representative Ushiba, something that people in Washington still talk about. The talks were extremely intense, but this confrontation of minds and wills produced strong feelings of mutual personal trust between the negotiators. Mr. Strauss subsequently left government service and returned to private law practice, operating in Washington as a powerful Democratic Party leader. Whenever we meet he praises Ambassador Ushiba for his personal charisma and speaks of the warm friendship that developed between the two during the course of the tariff negotiations.

In the summer of 1982, deliberations concerning agricultural products began to be held, based on the Strauss-Ushiba agree-

18

ment, but these deliberations became stalemated, with the American side pressing for liberalization of import restrictions on beef and citrus fruits and the Japanese unable to comply due to circumstances at home. The Americans persisted in taking up the problematic 13 remaining items on the restricted imports list at GATT meetings, and in July 1983, consultations were opened based on GATT Article 23, Section 1. Hence, the American attitudes regarding the trade imbalance was becoming more and more confrontational.

From October 1982 to the spring of 1984, talks were held on six different occasions to negotiate positions on beef and citrus products. The Americans held that "the philosophy that underlies the remaining import restrictions insisted on by Japan is totally inconsistent with the spirit of GATT" and called upon Japan to "quickly abolish these import restrictions." In response, the Japanese continued to maintain that "in view of the relative importance of livestock production and the citrus industry to Japanese agriculture, liberalization in these areas is out of the question." Thus the negotiations stalled, with no prospect of resolution. Faced with this adamant Japanese attitude, the Americans came to see beef and citrus fruits as symbolic of the closed nature of Japanese markets. Continuing demands to open the Japanese markets to U.S. exports made a bad situation worse.

During the course of these negotiations, the Americans came to the conclusion that their demand for "liberalization," in the sense of the complete and immediate abolition of the import guidelines, was too shocking to the Japanese, and that this was causing the negotiations to bog down unnecessarily. In private conversations they revised their stance, saying "our use of the term 'liberalization' was a mistake. What we are really saying is that you should change your import guidelines so that they are nearly free and unlimited." However, the Japanese continued to reject the American demands for sharply expanding the import guidelines.

In January 1984, the Japanese came to believe that some kind of practical resolution should be reached before the Ushiba-Strauss agreement lapsed in March of the same year. The new position was that, although full liberalization could not be seriously entertained, it would be necessary to consider some degree of expansion in the import guidelines contingent on prevailing market conditions.

Many within the Japanese government began to believe that negotiations should be conducted at the political level, with the Agriculture Minister making a visit to the United States, in order to encourage a compromise settlement. But too many conflicting political interests were involved, and the minister's U.S. visit became doubtful. Nevertheless, in late March, Agriculture Minister Shinjiro Yamamura made the visit, taking with him three other influencial Diet members involved in the agriculture industry (Tsutomu Hata, Tokuichiro Tamazawa, and Shuji Kita) to represent the Liberal Democratic Party (LDP). These men entered into final negotiations with Trade Representative Brock, recognizing that the import guidelines would be expanded. But the reluctance of both the Japanese and the Americans to make concessions still precluded any compromise agreement, and the negotiations floundered, unable to resolve a difference of several hundred tons. "As hard as we have tried, we have been unable to reach a final conclusion in these negotiations," said Yamamura. "Accordingly, we are obliged to suspend the Washington talks and reopen the negotiations at some later date. In the meantime, our only recourse is to seek to make some domestic adjustments." (There was actually a scene where Yamamura explained his position to the media.)

At this point, with negotiations broken off at this high level, both the Japanese and the Americans knew that it would be impossible to reopen the negotiations and consider further concessions. *However,* Mr. Yamamura and the LDP representatives wanted somehow to urge the Americans to reconsider, and the Japanese government came to believe that a more resolute expansion of the guidelines would be beneficial to Japan-U.S. relations on the whole and in the interest of further expanding and developing agricultural trade. After consulting with Mr. Yamamura and his advisers, I visited Mr. Brock at his home and talked with him alone, offering him a little higher import quota for certain U.S. agricultural products. The Americans gave us their final answer that very night, and agreement was reached suddenly on April 8. (When I visited Mr. Brock on the afternoon of April 6, he had just been putting fertilizer on some rose seedlings. He washed his hands and invited me inside, saying, "I've been so busy with the negotiations, I haven't had a chance to take care of the garden.")

The agreement called for a number of items to be accomplished

20

within four years, or by fiscal 1987, including (1) increasing the import volume of high-grade beef by 27,600 tons by 1987, (2) increasing the import quota on fresh oranges every year by 11,000 tons, (3) increasing the import quota on orange juice every year by 500 tons, and (4) abolishing the guidelines on grapefruit juice in fiscal 1986, and after implementing import quotas for two years, adjusting according to domestic demand. In other words, the import quotas on beef and oranges would be raised by degrees each year until, after four years, they would be double the 1983 levels.

With the resolution of the beef-and-orange problem, which had become emblematic of Japan's closed market, the Japanese believed they had overcome a major obstacle to the open-market policy, and the focus of American trade negotiations with Japan shifted to manufactured goods. Under the leadership of Vice President George Bush, who was given overall responsibility for handling relations with Japan, the administration in Washington worked hard to support the progress made during President Reagan's visit to Japan, and hailed this accord as a landmark in the government's Japan policy (along with the yen-dollar report which was issued at the end of May). As the country geared up for the presidential election, this success also had great political significance in the United States.

One humorous incident occurred when the negotiations on beef and oranges were not going well, and Senator Baucus (Democrat from Montana) organized a "beef day" in the Senate dining room. The Japanese ambassador and members of his staff were invited, along with several congressmen and a gaggle of media representatives.

The purpose of this event was clearly to put pressure on Japan to increase beef imports from the United States.

One clever embassy staff member got hold of some small flags used in Japanese supermarkets. The flags said "Beef Sale Day." We took these along to the dining room, together with a large number of bottles of the soy sauce that the Kikkoman Company had been producing in Wisconsin for about ten years.

Confronted by the demonstration urging Japan to buy more beef, we countered with the following announcement. "It is said that inexpensive American beef can't get into Japan because of

21

our closed markets, and that Japanese consumers are obliged to purchase more expensive products. We want you to know that we are working very hard to increase beef consumption, however, as you can see by these flags." At this point we brought out the Kikkoman bottles. "Now, we have some soy sauce here that is made from soybeans grown in the American midwest and produced by American workers in a Japanese factory in Wisconsin. Put some of this on the roast beef that you are being served here, and it will taste a lot better." This announcement produced a roar of laughter.

"Beef day" could have been a very awkward experience for us, but our little counterdemonstration completely changed the mood of the gathering, and subsequent dealings between Senator Baucus and me became very friendly.

3

Japanese-American Relations and Politics

At the beginning of 1985, the trade-friction problem with Japan was just about to boil over. On March 28 the Senate passed the "Japan Retaliation Resolution" by a unanimous vote of 92 to zero. This was followed on April 2 by the passage through the Senate Finance Committee of the "Japan Retaliation Bill," which would make the earlier resolution legally binding. On the same day the House of Representatives adopted a similar "Japan Retaliation Resolution" by the overwhelming majority of 394 to 19. The problems of economic friction are always serious, but whereas the situation was relatively mild in 1984, (judging by sparse coverage), things began to heat up early in 1985, and Japan was subjected to rather shrill criticism. Our response was generally one of surprise at this dramatic change, which left everyone perplexed. The previous year had been an election year in America, and some observers had thought that Japan-U.S. economic problems might have become a campaign issue for the first time in U.S. politics. That those problems did not become a campaign issue is due largely to the effects of President Reagan's visit to Japan in November 1983. At that time, the prevailing view in America was that the president should use the occasion to put pressure on the Japanese to correct the worsening Japan-U.S. trade imbalance. The president, however, was wary of embarrassing the government of an allied nation and he sought to suppress the dissenting opinion of those high-ranking officials in the executive branch who were critical of Japan. (Needless to say, this posture was reinforced by the "Ron-Yasu" relationship between the president and the prime minister.)

23

In January 1983, Prime Minister Nakasone visited the United States, engaging in talks with the president and reconfirming the solidarity of the Japan-U.S. alliance. Nakasone went to the Williamsburg Summit and played an active role in dealing with the issues on that agenda, including Japan-U.S. trade problems. It was during this period that a personal relationship of trust developed between Prime Minister Nakasone and President Reagan. At the summit, Nakasone participated actively in drafting a political declaration that argued for the strengthening of Western solidarity. The Americans were very appreciative of Nakasone's efforts. Then when the Korean Air Lines 747 was shot down by the Soviets, the Japanese government provided information to the United States that the Japanese Self Defense Forces had gathered (even at the expense of Japanese security). This enabled the United States to confidently make its case before the UN Security Council, and made America more confident of Japanese cooperation. President Reagan's efforts to avoid creating difficulties for Prime Minister Nakasone can also be seen in the handling of the Houdaille suit mentioned in the preceding chapter.

During his visit to Japan, Reagan limited his comments to general statements concerning Japan-U.S. cooperation in maintaining free trade and opposing protectionism, but did not get into any of the concrete issues. The statements published in the media after the talks also held to this line.

Reagan's visit was roundly hailed as a great success, and was said to be of monumental significance for Japan-U.S. relations. However, with the trade deficit vis-à-vis Japan for fiscal 1983 sure to go over $20 billion, circumstances demanded that the achievements of the Japan visit be followed up with concrete measures.

It was in this context that the president gave Vice President George Bush overall responsibility for carrying on relations with Japan. Thus it fell to Bush to take the lead in negotiating with Japan, while exercising vice-presidential influence over various departments within the administration.

In Japan, meanwhile, Mr. Toshio Komoto (Director General of the Economic Planning Agency) was given responsibility for domestic coordination, assisted by Foreign Minister Shintaro Abe, who would handle negotiations with the United States. Under the authority of these U.S. and Japanese officials, numerous efforts were undertaken to give concrete expression to President Reagan's Japan visit, including the meetings of the Japan-U.S. Trade Committee, Investment Committee, and Working Subcommittee on Energy, as well as industrial policy talks and other conferences. The NTT procurement decision was also postponed, and the compromise on agricultural products discussed in chapter 2 was finally reached.

Vice President Bush visited Japan in early May 1984, at which time there were again great hopes that some of the enduring problems could be resolved. During President Reagan's visit the previous year, agreement had been reached to hold special joint sessions to deal with the yen/dollar exchange rate. In late May the participants in these sessions finalized their efforts and issued a report. The Americans hailed this as an unprecedented development toward the liberalization of Japan's financial market and the internationalization of the Japanese yen.

With the presidential election coming up in November 1984, President Reagan's Republican administration sought to suppress domestic criticism concerning the significance of the president's Japan visit by pushing ahead with measures to coordinate Japan-U.S. economic relations, and by avoiding anti-Japanese statements or actions within the administration or the Republican party that would raise doubts in this regard.

Meanwhile, Walter Mondale (vice president under President Jimmy Carter) had declared his candidacy for the Democratic Party nomination, and was advocating protectionist positions — including support for local content legislation — and relentlessly repeated his condemnation of the trade deficit with Japan. Inside America, however, these declarations were often interpreted as Mondale's support for labor unions and other special interest groups. Mondale may have come to believe that attacking Japanese imports too vehemently might provoke the opposition of voters in general, who were enjoying the superior qualities of those imports and thus enriching their lives. In any event, he began to avoid making statements concerning Japan-U.S. trade problems. As the presidential race intensified, both the Republican and Democratic parties excluded Japan-U.S. trade friction as a campaign issue, for internal political reasons, and the media were relatively silent on the issue until the election was over.

Once the election was over, however, the high-ranking officials in the administration who had long been critical of Japanese behavior now felt at liberty to voice their opinions on the subject. In the fall it was reported that the United States would record the greatest trade deficit in its history in 1984, and that the deficit with Japan would also reach record proportions. The Department of Commerce announced its projection that the deficit with Japan would likely total around 30 billion dollars. Thus the deficit with Japan and the general problem of the trade imbalance gradually became matters of immediate concern to Congress (along with the associated problem of the fiscal deficit).

It was decided that Prime Minister Nakasone and President Reagan would meet for talks in Los Angeles on January 2, 1985. In preparation for this Japan-U.S. summit meeting, the Reagan administration held many cabinet-level conferences to decide what stance should be taken on the problem of the trade deficit with Japan. These conferences were said to be very serious and intense. According to later reports, the Trade Policy Committee (TPC) chaired by Trade Representative Brock and the Cabinet Council on Commerce & Trade (CCCT) chaired by Secretary of Commerce Baldridge held a joint session, during which intense criticism was leveled at Japan and there was spirited debate over what specific negotiation strategy the United States should pursue to persuade Japan to open its markets. The Commerce Department, pointing out that previous trade negotiations with Japan had not brought about increased exports of U.S. goods to Japan, argued tenaciously for pressing Japan to make a specific quantitative promise, such as to double American imports within three years or triple them within five years. At the Washington Embassy we got wind of what was happening, and immediately began airing strong counterarguments in all appropriate quarters, reasoning that there was no way in a market economy that we could make specific promises about import volumes, and that the Commerce Department's idea was impracticable.

In the end, this joint session failed to reach a consensus, and the Reagan administration assigned the formulation of Japan-trade policy to the Senior Inter-Governmental Group on International Economic Policy, headed by Treasury Secretary Donald Regan.

As a result of his experience in the Special Yen-Dollar Conference dealing with the problems of liberalizing Japan's financial market and internationalizing the yen, Donald Regan had come to certain conclusions similar to the yen-dollar report that had been issued in late May 1984. The importance of this report was: (1) that it presented a thorough-going analysis of the problems in Japan's financial market, from both a legal and a practical perspective, and (2) that it established specific goals for liberalizing the Japanese financial market and was conducive to Japanese consent. Accordingly, Regan proposed the adoption of a style of negotiation in which breakthroughs could be worked out in high-level talks, focusing on particular fields where it was believed that America had adequate export competitiveness but still could not penetrate the Japanese market because of various internal restrictions and impediments. Regan's idea was to abandon the conventional "package negotiation" style and apply the methods of the Special Yen-Dollar Committee to trade talks. The objective would be to achieve specific improvements through a "market-oriented sector-selective" (MOSS) approach in which specific fields were negotiated separately according to prevailing market conditions. After much study and debate, U.S. officials concluded that this approach should be employed in negotiating with Japan, and selected four specific fields, namely telecommunications, electronics, pharmaceuticals and medical equipment, and forestry products.

In January 1985, the Nakasone-Reagan summit meeting opened in Los Angeles. The official mood was marked by grave concern over the trade deficit, but the atmosphere in the meeting itself remained extremely cordial, bolstered by the mutual feelings of trust that had developed between the prime minister and the president — i.e., the "Ron-Yasu" relationship.

The summit meeting was preceded by a breakfast meeting between Foreign Minister Shintaro Abe and Secretary of State George Shultz. Trade relations between the two nations were discussed at this earlier meeting, but Abe and Shultz also exchanged views on the broader international situation, and the breakfast was marked by a high degree of mutual accord. This was not surprising, perhaps, as it was the sixteenth time the two men had met. Secretary Shultz explained how seriously the United States viewed the problems of economic friction. Foreign Minister Abe responded by emphasizing how earnestly the Japanese government was working to open its markets, and explained how Japan's internal circumstances made it difficult to lower the import duties on lumber products.

When the summit meeting itself got underway, Prime Minister Nakasone took the initiative in setting forth problems from the Japanese side, an approach adopted deliberately to avoid being put immediately on the defensive. The prime minister recognized that Japan and the United States were faced with many economic problems, and emphasized that the Japanese government would work even harder than it had in the past to open Japan's markets and to support free trade. While noting his appreciation for Nakasone's remarks, President Reagan urged the Japanese to take even more strenuous measures to open their markets, particularly in view of the highly charged mood of Congress and other groups within the United States. The president proposed that negotiations start as early as possible in the four designated fields in order to begin resolving the problems. Nakasone replied that Japan was willing to negotiate within the MOSS framework, but said that due to domestic circumstances there would still be great difficulties in making concessions regarding lumber products.

A luncheon followed, at which Treasury Secretary Regan complained that the kidney dialysis machine made by the Baxter Travenol Company was not widely used in Japan because of restrictions imposed by the Ministry of Health and Welfare. The prime minister responded that he had been fully apprised of this U.S. grievance, impressing the Americans with his thorough grasp of the issues.

More than half of the Abe-Shultz meeting had been devoted to SDI (Strategic Defense Initiative) considerations, and in the summit meeting President Reagan himself emphasized that SDI involved non-nuclear defensive weapons, explaining that "the research and development of such defensive weapons is a moral obligation which the United States must fulfill in the interests of world peace." Prime Minister Nakasone responded that he could understand the need for SDI research.

After the summit ended, the two leaders read prepared press statements to American and foreign journalists, praising the achievements of the high-level talks. In his remarks, Nakasone emphasized that "both Japan and the United States would continue to work together very diligently for world peace and prosperity, building on the 'three supports' [of trust, responsibility, and friendship]." Reagan characterized the meetings as "a reconfirmation of the close and friendly ties that bind our two great peoples and of the democratic values which we share." I think these statements indeed express the significance of the Los Angeles talks as Japan and America looked ahead to the Bonn Summit scheduled for May.

Although the four-field negotiating structure was agreed upon at the Los Angeles meeting, no decisions were made as to the timing of the negotiations or as to what conclusions they might reach.

Before leaving the Los Angeles Summit, I want to digress for a moment and relate a particular episode which took place there.

The Abe-Shultz breakfast talk was followed by separate talks, then the formal meeting of the two leaders, and finally the luncheon. As the luncheon was nearing its conclusion, President Reagan said, "The trouble is that American businesses just aren't working hard enough to penetrate the Japanese market." And this, he said, reminded him of a story.

During a flood, a man had climbed up onto the roof of his house. A rowboat came by, then a motorboat, and finally a helicopter, all offering to save the fellow. But he stubbornly refused each offer, saying "God will save me." Eventually the flood waters rose and carried the man away. The fellow drowned of course, and when he got to heaven he said to the Lord, "After I believed in you so strongly, why didn't you save me?" "What do you mean?" replied the Lord, "I sent boats and even a helicopter to save you!"

The president told this parable without further comment. Nobody asked him what it meant, and nobody knew what his purpose was in telling it. All we can do now is to speculate. According to one interpretation, Ronald Reagan sees himself as initiating various measures to preserve free trade, but believes that the raging tides of protectionism will sweep all before it if others do not respond promptly to his initiatives. In other words, Reagan seems to be saying, "Look, I am working hard on this, but you Japanese can't just depend on me. You've got to work hard too." Perhaps that is what the story means.

4

A Change in Negotiating Style

We need to take a closer look at the market-oriented sector-selective (MOSS) approach to negotiations that was mentioned in chapter 3.

According to the U.S. interpretation, *market-oriented* implies that sales volumes are determined by natural supply-and-demand relationships, with no artificially imposed impediments, while *sector-selective* means that appropriate fields should be selected, rather than individual products, and that talks should then be conducted to remove the obstacles to trade within these fields.

The fields of telecommunications, electronics, medical equipment and pharmaceuticals, and forestry products were chosen, reportedly because in each case the market in Japan is large, the future potential is great, U.S. competitiveness is strong, and the field is well-defined.

In the background of America's proposal of the MOSS approach was the fact that, despite Japan's announcements of one open-market policy after another (each one having been hammered out with great difficulty), no sooner was one obstacle in the Japanese marketplace removed than another was encountered. The Americans would persuade the Japanese to relax or abolish certain import guidelines, for example, only to run up against high import duties. If the duties were reduced, there were then the problems of meeting standards and obtaining certifications. And looming behind all these problems were the ever-present Japanese cartels.

Given such circumstances as these, the removal of one or two barriers resulted in no substantial increase in U.S. exports to Japan. I think what the Americans were after was something like the former Yen-Dollar Committee, where the United States and Japan would sit down calmly together, thoroughly discuss the individual trade barriers in realistic terms, and arrive at workable solutions.

The Americans explained that unless they could create the impression in the United States that this approach was working well, the administration would not be able to prevail against the tide of protectionism that was gathering strength in Congress.

Less than ten days had passed since the Los Angeles talks when the United States sent a delegation to Tokyo, headed by Under Secretary of State W. Allen Wallis, to request that negotiations in the four fields get started.

At this point the Japanese hurriedly began to set up studies on the four fields in various ministries, and were also faced with the urgent need to prepare for the reconvening of the Diet at the end of January. With their agenda so full already, Japanese officials were in a quandary as to how to respond to the sudden American initiative. In the first place, the Japan-U.S. High-Level Conference was to open sometime in March, together with the Japan-U.S. Trade Committee, a subordinate body. The schedule for these meetings had already been tentatively worked out, and now the Japanese had to worry about how this would fit in with the timing of the four-field talks that the Americans were anxiously requesting.

The Americans were very keen on convening meetings in January, and insisted that these meetings be on the deputy-minister level. Government officials in Japan wanted to conclude the high-level conference before the deliberations of the Budget Committee of the Diet got underway, and so agreed to meet the Americans in Tokyo at the end of January, but this allowed far too little time for internal coordination.

The American delegation headed by Under Secretary of State Wallis had Deputy Trade Representative Smith as second in command. Other members included Under Secretary of Commerce Lionel Olmer, Assistant Secretary of Agriculture Daniel Amstutz, and Assistant Secretary of Treasury David Mulford. The Japanese negotiators included vice ministers from the Agriculture, Forestry and Fisheries, the Health and Welfare, and the Posts and Telecommunications ministries. This was in one sense an unprecedented meeting for the Japanese, who ordinarily conduct such negotiations at the bureau-chief level (assistant secretary level).

31

The meetings were thus put together, but in terms of content the Japanese refused to move one step beyond the existing framework and assumed an extremely passive posture throughout. Or at least the American delegates took it that way, returning to Washington with very obvious dissatisfactions that they made widely known.

The Americans were particularly anxious to resolve the problems that existed in the telecommunications field before the Nippon Telegraph & Telephone Public Corporation became officially privatized on April 1. Their anxieties in this regard further amplified their frustrations with Japan.

The second round of negotiations was conducted in mid-February, but the deliberations concerning telecommunications became increasingly bogged down in detail, causing the American negotiators to become more and more dissatisfied.

The United States is the most advanced nation in the world in the fields of advanced technology, and in the view of the U.S. negotiators it is surpassingly competitive in the field of telecommunications — a field where there is tremendous growth potential in the Japanese market. Keenly aware of this, the American negotiators felt that to make too many compromises and concessions would be to invite very serious trouble further down the road. I think that it was out of this uncommonly strong crisis mentality that their frustrations with the Japanese arose.

In the past, Japan had promised the United States on numerous occasions that it would implement two principles, namely "domestic/foreign non-discrimination" and "procedural transparency," based on new telecommunications operations legislation. The United States was mainly concerned with how these principles would be specifically implemented at the level of legal enforcement. Why? Because the Americans were all too aware of the fierce power struggle that had developed between MITI and the Ministry of Posts and Telecommunications (MPT) over value added network (VAN) standards, and thus felt that it would be far from adequate just to have the two principles spelled out in some legislative act. They were very conscious of the need to have the two principles embodied in specific governmental directives, and indeed in the fine details of ministerial orders, so that there would be absolutely no loopholes that would allow obscure discretionary actions to be taken at the administrative level. The United

States objected vehemently to the setting up of both notification and registration procedures in order to conduct VAN operations, fearing that a registration system would provide grounds for discrimination against foreign companies at the discretion of administrative officials.

Administrative Vice Minister of Posts and Telecommunications Koyama visited Washington toward the end of February and conducted talks with some of the American officials. Through these talks Japan came to a direct "recognition" of both the sense of crisis felt by the Americans and their awareness of the problems involved. This was extremely significant in promoting further negotiations. Subsequently, Under Secretary of Commerce Olmer visited Japan, after which Koyama made a second trip to Washington to finalize the negotiations, and a compromise settlement was reached which satisfied the U.S. administration. I think that the problem became as difficult as it did because of the strong suspicions of the Americans, and because of their preoccupation with worries that they would fall behind Japan in advanced technological fields.

Another factor that complicated the negotiations was the turf struggle that developed between the trade representative team and the Commerce Department. The United States had sent Deputy Trade Representative Smith and Under Secretary of Commerce Olmer to act as co-chairmen in conducting talks with the Japanese during the January negotiations on telecommunications, but Olmer took over this leadership role by himself in subsequent negotiations, reflecting the struggle that was going on behind the scenes.

The second problem was in the field of electronics, concerning which the U.S. negotiators might not have been very well prepared at the January negotiations. The Japanese were ready to entertain any specific problems which the Americans brought up, but the latter did not make any specific proposals until March. And the Japanese were prepared to promote technological exchange and investment in this field, just as they had quickly agreed, for example, to a reciprocal abolition of import duties on semiconductors. Incidently, it had taken the U.S. administration more than a year longer to get congressional approval on abolishing duties on semiconductors than it had taken the Japanese government to get Diet approval.

The third area of contention was in the field of pharmaceuticals and medical equipment. When the Baxter Travenol Company approached officials in the Ministry of Health and Welfare (MHW) informally, the ministry made it very clear that it would handle the case differently than before, temporarily appeasing Baxter Travenol's apprehension. With this episode in the background, there was optimism concerning the potential progress of the negotiations in this field, but the toughest problem arose in determining whether or not foreign clinical test data should be universally accepted. MHW officials had taken a negative position on this, arguing that there were physiological differences between the Japanese and the peoples of other nations, so that the use of foreign pharmaceuticals based on foreign data could lead to a public health problem in Japan. In contrast the Americans had strongly insisted that such an approach would not be acceptable internationally. During the negotiations the Japanese modified their position, saying they would accept foreign clinical test data except for medications requiring direct administration, so some progress was made.

In Washington I also got an earful of complaints from acquaintances and others concerned about pharmaceutical exports. A human being was a human being, they argued — so the Japanese insistence on differences in body type was outrageous. I would counter by explaining that with medicines for colds or digestive disorders the dosages prescribed for Americans were too strong for the Japanese and sometimes produced side effects. I would even cite specific examples, but the response was always pretty much the same — scornful laughter.

Turning to the final problem of forestry products, for a long time U.S. officials had been pressing hard for Japan to lower its customs duties on plywood and composite board materials. The duties on the latter had been lowered slightly two years earlier, but a recession was hurting the domestic industry, and we had to keep explaining that it was impossible under the circumstances to make the drastic cuts that the Americans wanted.

Just before his visit to Japan in November 1983, President Reagan made a speech to lumber industry leaders in Washington State promising them that he would work hard to get lower duties. This statement was accepted throughout the United States as a political promise, and it signaled that the administration was now taking a stronger posture toward the problem.

In February 1985, I paid a visit to Montana State University, the alma mater of Mike Mansfield, the U.S. Ambassador to Japan, on the occasion of the inauguration of the Mansfield Memorial Lectures. Traveling with me from Washington, D.C., was Senator Max Baucus. At a press conference held at the Missoula airport, Baucus strongly appealed to his fellow Montanans by calling vigorously for lower duties on plywood. A large amount of plywood is exported to Japan from Washington, Oregon, and Montana, so the concern in that region about this problem is considerable. Senator Bob Packwood of Oregon had just been appointed chairman of the Senate Finance Committee. Taking everything into consideration, I think that Japan-U.S. trade in forestry products is becoming an increasingly political issue.

5

An Impatient Congress

In the 1984 elections, the Republican Party lost Senator Charles
Percy (chairman, Foreign Relations Committee) of Illinois and
Senator Roger Jepsen (chairman, Joint House-Senate Finance
Committee) in election defeats, and gained one new Senate seat.
This gave the Republicans a total of 53 seats in the Senate to the
Democrats 47, and set the stage for vigorous congressional bat-
tles. In addition, the decision of Majority Leader Howard Baker
of Tennessee not to run for reelection and the election defeat of
Foreign Relations Committee Chairman Percy made it necessary
for the Republicans to put together a new group of Senate party
leaders.

The list of possible successors to the post of majority leader
was narrowed down to Senator Robert Dole of Kansas and Senator Ted Stevens of Alaska, with the final vote going to Dole by
a very slim margin. Dole was succeeded in the Finance Committee chairmanship by Senator Bob Packwood of Oregon, and
Senator Lugar of Indiana took over the chairmanship of the
Foreign Relations Committee vacated by Percy. As the ranking
Republican on the Foreign Relations Committee, right-wing Senator Jesse Helms of North Carolina would most likely have been
appointed chairman of that committee had he so desired, but
Helms — coming off of a hard-won reelection bid against former
Governor Hunt of North Carolina (who was backed by agricultural interest groups) — announced that he would retain his chair-
manship of the Agriculture, Nutrition, and Forestry Committee.

Majority Leader Dole was expected to run for president in
1988, and some intense internal struggles had gone on in the
formation of the Senate Republican leadership. Not surprisingly,

then, Dole's relationship with the Reagan administration was not exactly one of complete cooperation. On the contrary, Dole was said to be anxious to demonstrate his independence so as to better position himself for the presidential election. Finance Committee Chairman Packwood's positions were also often felt to be critical of the Reagan administration.

The House leadership, meanwhile, continued to be dominated by Thomas (Tip) O'Neill, Democrat from Massachusetts. O'Neill was 74 years old, however, and for a while the age issue gave rise to rumors of the leadership being ceded to the next generation. In the 1984 elections, the Democrats captured more than 250 of the 435 seats in the House of Representatives, and thus continued to enjoy a 70-seat majority over the Republicans, so it was commonly believed that O'Neill's successor would be decided without real opposition.

There was strong demand from within the Democratic Party, particularly from its southern wing, for a younger Speaker of the House. Representative Charles Stenholm of Texas ran for the position in opposition to O'Neill, but the situation became very confused, because of fears that the party image had suffered badly after the humiliating defeat of Walter Mondale in 1984. As a result, forces within the party began to operate in favor of "unity and solidarity," and O'Neill was reelected as Speaker of the House after announcing that he would retire from politics at the end of 1986.

Hence both the Republican and Democratic parties were concerned with placing themselves in the most advantageous positions for the coming 1986 midterm elections and the 1988 presidential elections; this was certainly reflected in the way leadership was established in the Senate and House, respectively. This was no longer the Congress of a former generation in which House and Senate party leaders controlled the party member votes, and policy was determined and hammered out as the final will of Congress along predictable party lines.

As the 99th Congress began its work in January, the greatest problem it faced was that of how to deal with a national deficit that had reached colossal proportions. Aided by Reaganomics, the U.S. economy had been steadily recovering, but the deficit became progressively worse year after year, reaching the staggering figure of $220 billion in fiscal 1984. Despite various White House statements on this issue, it is undeniable that the deficit resulted in high interest rates, which in turn led to a strong dollar on international currency markets.

In the ensuing debates concerning possible corrective measures, the Democrats concentrated on reducing defense spending, maintaining their traditional opposition to cuts in social welfare funding.

The Republican administration, however, has steadfastly refused to respond to demands to cut the defense budget, championing an approach to the deficit problem that emphasized cuts in social welfare spending. These conflicting positions have resulted in a continuous head-on confrontation between the administration and Congress.

In preparing its proposal for the 1986 federal budget, the administration announced that it would hold the 1986 deficit down to $185 billion, reduce this by an additional $50 billion a year thereafter, and get it down to $144 billion by 1990. Congress reacted strongly to this announcement, however, and Majority Leader Dole called for Senate Republicans to draft their own budget proposal, saying that as things stood in January it would be impossible to get congressional approval for the administration's proposal. This idea was rejected by Senate Republicans, however, reportedly because agreement could not even be reached within the party to begin work on drafting a separate proposal.

Confronted by the federal deficit as the biggest domestic issue in U.S. politics, Congress had no choice but to try and resolve it, but they were having a terrible time in coming up with any specific ways of combatting the problem. This issue was frustrating enough, but it was further complicated by the closely related problem of the trade deficit. Since January, the administration had been experiencing frustrations in the Tokyo trade negotiations. When these frustrations were vented during the congressional hearings that were held in February and March, the exasperation of Congress was even further intensified.

We saw an expression of this congressional exasperation in the speech of Senator Richard Lugar, chairman of the Senate Foreign Relations Committee, at the National Press Club in Washington on January 23, in which he denounced Japan in no uncertain terms. This was very surprising, given Lugar's hitherto moderate position on the issue. On March 8, however, the tense mood in Congress virtually exploded when Chairman John Danforth (Republican from Missouri) and others on the Senate Finance Committee's Trade Subcommittee followed one another in leveling very harsh criticism against Japan.

So harsh was their language, that it prompted Senators Spark Matsunaga (Democrat, Hawaii) and Bill Bradley (Democrat, New Jersey) to caution the subcommittee members against the danger of "forgetting the lessons of history."

It was shortly after this that I visited Senator Danforth to say good-bye as I was leaving my post in Washington. He met me in his office and had the following to say:

> I have supported free trade up until now, and I don't plan to change my position on that in the future. Japan, however, has been continually telling us that it was going to open its markets, and every time the Japanese make an announcement about their so-called open-market policy, the Americans welcome this appreciatively, and expect that it will lead to really open markets. In actuality, however, exports of American products to Japan are not growing. Faced with this fact, we can only conclude that Japan's open-market policy is just talk, having no real substance.
>
> Many people have come from Japan to Washington to explain to us the situation in Japan, and to make excuses, but I for one am sick and tired of hearing these excuses. Meeting with the Japanese, therefore, is just a waste of time, and so I have decided not to meet with them anymore. I am meeting with you, Ambassador Okawara, because our acquaintance goes back a ways, and because you say you are leaving your post here in Washington, but I have no intention of listening to more Japanese arguments.

When I asked "What do you intend to do then?," Senator Danforth's facial expression became severe. "All we can do is retaliate," he replied without hesitation.

"Do you know what retaliation will mean?" I asked. "I hope you will give some thought to the severe effect it will have on the world economy, and on the U.S. economy itself, if the United States adopts protectionist trade policies." I sought to persuade the Senator with various arguments, and urged him to change

his mind, but he was adamant, and refused to budge from his position.

On another occasion I also visited Senator Lloyd Bentsen, the Democratic Senator from Texas, to pay my parting respects. Bentsen's language was not as harsh as Danforth's, but he also expressed his "lost patience with the failure of Japan's open-market policies to yield real results, as typified in the beef and orange problems." I called on other congressmen at this time, and they all received me politely and spoke words of appreciation, but the atmosphere became tense every time the issue of Japan-U.S. trade was raised.

Wishing to say good-bye to President Reagan I requested the State Department to arrange such an opportunity. I received the reply that there was no precedent for a president to receive a departing foreign ambassador.

In Japan, retiring foreign ambassadors are treated with extreme courtesy by both the Imperial Household and the government, and I felt certain that my request was fully justified on the basis of bilateral reciprocity. So I contacted Chief of Staff Donald Regan and National Security Advisor McFarlane and told them how I felt about the matter. Having had very friendly relationships with each of these men, they took the matter in hand and I received word that same day that the president would make time to see me on March 11. When I went to the White House at the appointed hour, news had been received just that morning of the new appointment of Mikhail Gorbachev as General Secretary of the Soviet Communist Party, and the President's working office was humming with administration officials apparently discussing this new development in relation to U.S. policy toward the Soviet Union. I waited for 15 minutes in the adjacent Roosevelt Room chatting with National Security Council staff aide Guston Sigur. The Roosevelt Room is so called because of the oil painting of Theodore Roosevelt hanging in it, along with the bronze statue of the "rough-riding" Roosevelt on horseback and the bust of Franklin D. Roosevelt which also decorate the chamber.

The White House staff was apparently discussing the question of whom should be sent to attend the funeral of the late Chairman Chernenko. The administration had for some time been interested in improved relations with the Soviets, and particularly in holding a U.S.-Soviet summit meeting. The morning newspapers carried stories urging the president to attend the funeral himself, to take advantage of the occasion to conduct some timely condolence diplomacy, and call for a summit meeting with the new Soviet leader. While some commentators said the president should go, others argued that it was traditional for the vice president to attend the funerals of foreign heads of state. Vice President Bush had just concluded a visit to Africa, and was at the moment in Geneva for the March 12 reopening of the U.S.-Soviet arms reduction talks after a long hiatus.

When I was invited into the president's office, Secretary of State George Shultz, Chief of Staff Donald Regan, and the president's Special Advisor on National Security Robert McFarlane all greeted me and retired from the room.

In accord with Washington protocol for receiving foreign dignitaries, the president sat on the sofa at the left of the fireplace, and I was directed to sit on the sofa on the right. Regan, Sigur, and Presidental Assistant Pierpont were also on hand for the occasion. After I paid my parting respects, President Reagan thanked me for my work in Washington, and then touched on the subject of Japan-U.S. economic relations, insisting on the necessity to work together in combatting protectionism and protecting free trade.

"I have continued to support free trade and oppose the moves in Congress toward protectionism," said the president. "And this position is not going to change one bit in the future. But I am very distressed by the recent vehement mood of the Congress. Upon your return to Japan, I hope you will convey my feelings to Prime Minister Nakasone and the Japanese people."

In terms of official Washington protocol, this was an unprecedented meeting. I think probably that Regan and McFarlane moved to set up the meeting after deciding that it could be beneficial to convey the president's feelings directly to the primary Japanese channels through the returning ambassador.

Even given what has been said, however, there is still the question of why Congress has become as exasperated with Japan as it has. I have already alluded in this chapter, in part, to some of the reasons and background issues. At the risk of being repetitious, I believe that the reasons can be summarized under the following three points.

There is first the fact that, despite the six market liberalization decisions that were announced by the Japanese government between 1982 and December 1984, the U.S. trade deficit with Japan continues to increase. This deficit was $18.1 billion in 1981, and by 1984 it was up to $36.8 billion, doubling in just three years. This has left Americans wondering what good to them all the open-market measures Japan has taken thus far have been, and has given rise to suspicions among Americans that the Japanese have been deceiving them. These suspicions intensified until, after the presidential elections and the announcement of the sharp increase in the deficit with Japan for 1984, they reacted with tremendous emotional force.

Second, there is a sense of being victimized as well as the enduring crisis mentality that permeates the industries and labor forces in areas where America competes with Japan. These feelings are communicated forcefully to Congress through effective lobbying activities.

There are a number of so-called caucuses in Congress which represent particular interests, such as textiles, steel, or automobiles. Steered by certain powerful figures in Congress — such as Senator John Heinz (Republican, Pennsylvania) in the case of steel, Senator Carl Levin and Representative John Dingell (both Democrats from Michigan) in the case of automobiles, and Senator Strom Thurmond (Republican, South Carolina) in the case of textiles — these caucuses bring tremendous political pressure to bear while protecting and supporting favored U.S. industries.

There is, in the third place, the fact that before congressional hearings the administration's trade representatives have vented their frustrations concerning the lack of progress in the four-field negotiations with Japan. This explicit dissatisfaction and exasperation with the negotiating positions of the Japanese reinforced the suspicions that were already being felt in Congress, making the atmosphere that much more volatile.

There are other reasons besides these which I could adduce. For example, finding a way to conquer the colossal fiscal deficit is the biggest issue now facing the Congress, but any move to either cut spending or increase taxes is expected to be met with strong domestic opposition, making no real solution seem possible. In seeking an outlet for the frustrations building up because of this impasse, the enormous trade deficit with Japan is a very convenient issue, representing the most conspicuous segment of the international trade deficit. Further encouraging this attitude is the growing belief among Americans that the Japanese do not play by the rules, that they go all out in promoting their own exports, while raising a variety of barriers to effectively discourage imports.

These pent-up frustrations finally burst forth at the end of March in the Danforth resolution (a resolution to retaliate against Japan) passed by the Senate Finance Committee, debated on the Senate floor, and adopted by unanimous vote. This resolution does not have the force of law, but the 92-to-0 vote—unprecedented for this type of resolution—expresses the collective will of the Senate, and represents a great blow to the Japanese.

Concerning the 92-to-0 vote, however, the off-the-record comments of one Senator are very instructive. He stated that there were two reasons for voting for this resolution. One was to send a message to the administration. Fundamentally, trade problems are within the jurisdiction of Congress, based on which the actual conduct of negotiations with foreign powers is left up to the executive branch. Currently, however, in the eyes of the Congress, the administration's negotiations with Japan are extremely unsatisfactory. The Danforth resolution sent a signal to the administration to produce results in its negotiations with Japan that more closely approximate senatorial expectations.

The second reason is that the resolution also sends a message to Japan. Japan enjoys the benefits of free trade to the fullest, and yet reneges on its obligations to promote imports. As long as this situation persists, the Congress of the United States will have no other recourse but to take retaliatory action against Japan. To obviate the need for such repugnant action, it is hoped that Japan will move quickly and decisively to correct the trade imbalances and to produce open-market results. This is the message of the unanimous vote, he said. At this stage, relatively few senators are contemplating immediate retaliatory measures.

Senator Packwood, chairman of the Finance Committee, on a separate occasion, explained it this way. "What we mean by retaliatory measures against Japan is not because of protectionism. These are simply measures which we will take because Japan does not open its markets."

Following this vote in the Senate, Congressman Dan Rostenkowski (Democrat, Illinois, chairman of Ways and Means Committee) sponsored a resolution that was adopted in the House of Representatives. The House resolution also called for Japan to open its markets, although using milder language than the Senate resolution. Sources close to Rostenkowski and to Sam Gibbons (Democrat, Florida, Trade Subcommittee chairman), who was also involved, explained off the record that these Congressmen felt that if they did not sponsor this resolution, Energy and Commerce Chairman John Dingell and others strongly critical of Japan might push a resolution through the House which would be worded even more severely than the Senate resolution.

Indeed, there are some Congressmen in the House who have steadfastly opposed the protectionist forces, including powerful members of the Trade Subcommittee, and in one sense the two resolutions can be interpreted as desperate measures to forestall a protectionist stampede in Congress or, perhaps, merely as early warnings of what might be to come. This is not to suggest for a moment, however, that the Japanese need not be very concerned. No matter how one looks at these developments, they still boil down to protectionism and to retaliation against Japan.

Speaking generally, I feel keenly that such champions of free trade as Rostenkowski, Gibbons, and Bill Frenzel (Republican, Minnesota) are beginning to feel helpless, in the sense that their arguments for free trade are losing their persuasive power in the face of trade imbalances that become worse with each passing year, and more particularly in the face of the steep curve that is being followed by the ongoing deterioration in trade relations with Japan. The fact that both houses of Congress now possess a condemnatory posture toward Japan lends further support to this view. The situation has become extremely worrisome.

It was against this background, on April 9, that the Japanese government announced a seventh round of open-market measures, redeclaring that plans for specific actions, including the reduction of customs duties, would be established by July. Prime Minister Nakasone himself appeared on television to explain to the Japanese people how serious the Japan-U.S. trade problems had become, and how imperative it was to promote imports. Such measures had never been taken before. Clips from Nakasone's television appearance were carried into homes all across the United States by the three major networks, and top coverage was given to the event in all major U.S. newspapers.

The Japanese measures were enthusiastically welcomed by President Reagan, Vice President Bush, White House Chief of Staff Regan, Trade Representative Brock, and others in the administration, who spoke publicly about their hopes that these new measures would soon provide substantive results.

The attitude of the administration, which had continually supported free trade and opposed protectionism, was one of honest expectancy. The Japanese government had now taken a positive step in favor of free trade, and was fulfilling its obligations by persuading its people to further open Japanese markets and reduce the trade surplus. The United States would now wait for the specific details of the Japanese plans to be worked out, fully expecting to see practical results.

The reaction of Congress, however, was much more guarded; I felt in fact that it was rather cool and severe. Senators Packwood (Finance Committee chairman) and Danforth (Trade Subcommittee chairman) spoke of the Japanese measures in dismissive terms. The issue was not a matter of announcements about foreign economic policy, they insisted, but rather a matter of specific actions and results. They warned that they would have to continue to be skeptical as things currently stood; uncertain as to whether the July action plans would produce any results or not.

With the Bonn Summit just over, Congress is presently in a relatively calm mood, at least on the surface, but I think we should pay close attention to how Congress interprets and responds to the implementation of the action plans.

In any event, it is becoming increasingly important that we further develop our contacts with Congress.

In the past, during the 1950s and early 1960s, the Washington Embassy was able to limit its activities to the consolidation of relations with the U.S. administration as represented by the State Department. Not much thought was given to developing broad direct contacts with Congress, either at the Japanese Embassy or other foreign embassies. Upon reflection, the power of the executive branch in those days was overwhelming, and congressional actions were largely controlled by the House and Senate leaderships. Once a few powerful Congressmen had determined their position on a given issue, that was the direction in which the entire federal legislature moved.

During the 1970s and early 1980s, however, this situation changed dramatically, partly due to the Vietnam War, the Watergate scandal, and various cases of corruption involving members of Congress. The House and Senate leaders lost much of their iron grip on their fellow members, and power within Congress became increasingly more diffused. At the same time, the balance of power between the executive and the legislature gradually shifted toward Congress, particularly with the passage and implementation of the controversial War Powers Act.

In response to these trends, the Japanese Embassy no longer limits its activities to the State Department, but now coordinates closely with presidential advisors, the office of the National Security Council, and various other departments of the executive offices. In addition, embassy personnel now maintain close, almost day-to-day, contact with certain key Congressmen and members of their staffs, providing them with information and otherwise seeking to enhance mutual understanding.

The brightest college graduates in the United States, unlike their Japanese counterparts, do not vie for positions in the government bureaucracy. But many of them do become lawyers or join the staffs of members of Congress in order to pave the way to future success. Quite a number of Congressmen now place great emphasis on drafting legislation and conducting investigations, for which purpose they employ appropriately talented persons. Many of these talented people use this congressional staff experience as stepping-stones to appointments to high positions in the administration, and many others become university professors or are recruited by research organizations and think tanks.

Assistant Secretary of Defense Richard Armitage (in charge of international affairs) was formerly on the staff of Senator Bob Dole, for example, while both Ambassador Robert Lighthizer at the office of the Trade Representative and Legal Advisor Claude Gingrich were on Dole's staff when he was the Senate Republican leader and chairman of the Finance Committee. Susan C. Schwab, who formerly worked at the U.S. Embassy in Tokyo, now plays a key role on the staff of Senator Danforth, a leader of the censure-Japan faction. Ms. Schwab is extremely well informed on the complexities of the Japanese economy.

The Japanese Embassy was once requested by Congress to testify before a congressional hearing. In view of its relationship to the administration, however, it would have been awkward and most improper for an ambassador or an embassy official to testify before Congress. On the other hand, it was important that Congress have a correct understanding of problems involving Japan, so we responded to the request by offering to participate in informal talks, stopping short of formal testimony. On numerous occasions thereafter the embassy exchanged views with members of Congress in such informal talks. The meetings held by Senator Percy (Foreign Relations Committee chairman), Congressman Clement Zablocki (House Foreign Relations Committee chairman), and Congressman de la Garza (House Agriculture Committee chairman) were specific examples of such talks. I believe these talks were very significant in promoting better mutual understanding.

In the 1986 midterm elections, one third of the seats in the Senate were up for election. This means that 22 Republican seats and 12 Democratic seats were at risk. Twenty-two of the current Republican Senators were elected in 1980, aided in their campaigns by the popularity of Ronald Reagan, or, as Americans say, "elected on Reagan's coattails."

Barred from a third term of office by an amendment to the U.S. Constitution, however, President Reagan would inevitably become a lame duck. Hence those facing reelection bids in 1986 could not pin their hopes on Ronald Reagan's influence. Consequently, those Republicans up for reelection in 1986 sought to gain support from their constituents by somehow positioning themselves independently from the president.

In the 1980 elections the Republican Party captured a majority in the Senate for the first time since 1954 (53 Republican seats to 47 Democratic). In the 1982 midterm elections, they increased their majority to 55 seats. In the 1984 elections they lost two seats, but still retained a narrow majority of 53 to 47. Several of the senatorial elections in 1984 were hotly contested, however, and some observers thought prior to the vote that the Senate majority would swing back to the Democrats.

It is evident that the Senate Republicans hoped to retain their majority in the 1986 elections and to carry this momentum right into the 1988 presidential elections. Having attained majority status and achieving the committee chairmanships which are prerogatives of that status, it was only natural that the Republicans should want to hold onto these positions and advantages.

Overshadowed by the problem of the federal deficit, the president nevertheless wanted a 5.9 percent net increase in the defense budget over the previous year's figure, but encountered rather stiff resistance in Congress (not limited to Democratic resistance) to his plans for holding down social welfare expenses. As noted earlier, Senator Robert Dole, the new leader of the Republican majority in the Senate and chairman of the Finance Committee, said that he would not be able to get Senate support for the 1986 budget being proposed by the administration and called for Senate Republicans to draft their own budget proposal. Dole's idea was scrapped, however, after Senate Republicans failed to reach a consensus, and no separate budget proposal was made. But there was a strong reaction against the administration's treatment of the defense budget as sacrosanct. Senate Republicans negotiated with the administration and eventually drafted a compromise proposal in which the net growth in defense spending was pared down to 3 percent. In a general session on May 2, however, while President Reagan was attending the 11th Summit Meeting in Bonn, the Senate rejected the compromise proposal and passed a modified budget proposal providing zero growth in defense spending (excluding allowances for inflation) by a vote of 51 to 48.

This was an unexpected development for Reagan, who had insisted that he would never compromise on an increase in defense spending, and it is possible to interpret the Senate's reaction as a response to a lame-duck presidency. The same may perhaps be said of a situation that developed with respect to the issue of trade policy in view of the international trade imbalance, the latter being seen as the twin specter of the federal deficit.

The Reagan administration has consistently opposed protectionism, and fundamental to its trade policies is the safeguarding of free trade. With the U.S. industrial world gripped in a crisis mentality, however, more and more members of Congress began to question the ability of the Reagan policies to safeguard the profits earned by U.S. corporations.

As of the end of 1984, the Japanese government had announced the implementation of market opening measures six times. Despite the administration's expectations, however, those measures did not result in increased U.S. exports to Japan — or so many in Congress suspected.

Indeed, contrary to the commonly held notions of many members of Congress, Japan not only imports farm goods and raw materials from the United States, but about half of its imports are manufactured goods. Looking at Japan's trade with the United States in 1984, imports of manufactured products were up 7.8 percent over the previous year, but Congressmen tended to focus only on the size of the trade deficit with Japan.

To summarize, the Senate Republican leaders, preoccupied with the 1986 midterm elections and aware of the approaching 1988 presidential elections, came to the conclusion that they could not conduct a winning campaign based on the results of previous trade policy and trade negotiations. This conviction took the form of harsh criticism against Japan, and it was a major factor underlying the adoption on March 28, by a vote of 92 to 0, of the resolution to retaliate against Japan that was sponsored by Senator Danforth.

It is interesting to note that those up for election in 1986 included Senators Bob Packwood (Finance Committee chairman), John Heinz, and Robert Dole (majority leader), while those facing election in 1988 included Senators John Danforth and John Chafee. These names all appear very prominently in newspaper coverage of Japan-U.S. trade problems.

Senator Danforth, chairman of the Trade Subcommittee, held a public hearing on March 8 dealing with the trade problems with Japan. At this hearing, Danforth and many other senators set forth arguments that condemned Japan. Danforth went so far as to say that "in order to bring the message home to the Japanese, an international conference should be held so that we can cooperate with the European Common Market and ASEAN nations in censuring Japan."

This prompted counterarguments from Democratic senators

Matsunaga (Hawaii) and Bradley (New Jersey), who said that Senator Danforth had "forgotten the lessons of history."

Senator Daniel Moynihan (Democrat, New York) also expressed his opinion at the hearing. "It is not fair to blame only Japan for the trade imbalance," argued Moynihan. "We ought rather to get at the real roots of the problem by dealing here at home with our federal deficit, our high interest rates, and the strong dollar." Later, in April, Congressman James Bates (Democrat, California) expressed opinions similar to those of Senator Moynihan in a paper he distributed to his fellow House members. Hence we need to remember that, in addition to those who censured Japan, there were also those in Congress who based their arguments on sounder judgment.

There are also Democrats in the Senate, such as Lloyd Bentsen (Texas), who is a powerful member of the Finance Committee, and Max Baucus (Montana), who have leveled harsh charges at Japan for its restrictions on beef imports and are probably known to many Japanese readers because of their frequent appearances in the newspapers.

The policy discord between the Reagan administration, which wants to persuade the Japanese and Europeans through trade talks to open their markets and thereby pave the way for increased exports of American manufactured goods, and the Senate Republicans, who questioned the viability of the current policies and point to the paucity of results so far, is providing excellent material for the Democrats to use in their attacks on the Republicans. According to some political analysts, the Democrats aligned themselves behind the Danforth proposal in order to drive a wedge between the Reagan administration and Senate Republicans, as well as to criticize Reagan's trade policies. In that sense, the argument of Senator Moynihan — calling for the United States to deal with its own fiscal deficit, high interest rates, and strong dollar — is in effect a criticism of the President's fiscal and trade policies.

We need to carefully evaluate the direction in which this whole scenario is moving as the United States approaches the midterm elections.

The question of how U.S. trade policy toward Japan is going to change not only involves the election-year politics of Congress, but will also be influenced by the specific measures taken by

Japan to open its markets. There is yet another critical factor, however, and that is the performance of the U.S. economy during 1986.

Thus far, the U.S. economy has exhibited a relatively solid recovery. According to projections, it was to trend favorably throughout 1985, and then begin slowing down slightly in 1986.

When real GNP grew only 0.7 percent in the first quarter (January–March) of 1985, some analysts began saying that the economy was decelerating.

Over the past two years, the early figures published for each quarter were eventually adjusted upward in every single case. However, the 2.1 percent growth projected for the first quarter of this year two months in advance was adjusted down to 1.3 percent one month later and then down to 0.7 percent when the final figures were published by the Department of Commerce on May 21.

In the background of these developments, the Federal Reserve Board reduced the official discount rate by 0.5 percent to 7.5 percent, exhibiting a cautious posture while it carefully monitored the trends in the economy. In the event that the economy stagnates just prior to the midterm elections in the fall of 1986, and the unemployment rate shoots up, the seriousness of Japan-U.S. trade problems will unavoidably intensify.

Thus the outcome of the 1986 midterm elections in the United States will have tremendous political and economic significance for Japan.

6

Direct Investment by Japan

Surprisingly few people are aware of the fact that, as of 1988 36 of America's 50 states maintained Japan liaison offices. When I mention this to people in the government and private industry, they always look very surprised.

Each of these 27 states is seeking to deepen its trade ties with Japan and is very anxious to attract direct investments by Japanese companies. This interest is also reflected in the liaison offices that have been established in Japan.

State governors from all over the United States have begun to make visits to Japan. Their primary objectives are to persuade the Japanese government and economic community to buy goods produced in their respective states and to deepen economic exchange by enticing Japanese businesses to come to those states.

In general, since World War II, the industrial center in the United States has been shifting from the East and Northeast toward the West and the so-called "Sunbelt" region of the South and Southwest. In demographic terms, St. Louis, Missouri, used to be considered the center of the U.S. population as well as the gateway to the west, but this center has now shifted due west to Kansas City, Kansas. The numbers of congressional voting districts allotted to each state are periodically revised, and the increase in this number for California and decrease for New York also testify to this population shift.

In the midst of these macro-level trends, the states in the southern and southwestern regions which have become centers for the high-tech and aerospace industries are seeking further economic development by aggressively enticing business ventures from Japan (particularly in view of the enormous economic power that Japan has been demonstrating). In the meantime, those states in the eastern and northeastern regions — the former industrial centers which have gradually lost their economic viability in the postwar era — have also begun to seek infusions of foreign capital.

A most extreme expression of this trend is seen in the holding of the Southeast United States-Japan Economic Conference. This conference was organized in 1976 as a result of a visit to Atlanta, Georgia, by an economic study group sent to tour the southeastern states by the Ministry of Foreign Affairs (MOFA) and headed by Norishige Hasegawa, chairman of Sumitomo Chemical Co., Ltd. George Busbee was the Governor of Georgia at the time, and was very enthusiastic about the conference. Rubin Askew — who served as Trade Representative during the Carter administration — also lent his influential support to the conference during his years as Governor of Florida.

This conference has grown steadily since its inception, with each annual meeting becoming a grander and more elaborate event. Tennessee has recently joined the initial membership of Georgia, Florida, North Carolina, South Carolina, Virginia, and Alabama. The states' enthusiasm for the conference is reflected in the attendance of all seven governors at the annual meetings.

Since the 1960s, quite a number of so-called Japan-regional U.S. economic societies have been formed, including the Japan-Hawaii Society, Japan-California Society, Japan-Texas Society, and Japan-Midwest Society. Consistent attendance by the governors of every state represented, however, is seen only in the case of the Japan-Midwest Society's conferences.

The initiatives made by these state governors in attracting Japanese industry have had impressive results. The number of Japanese companies which have set up operations in Georgia, for example, has now reached 123. This number includes such large corporations as Yoshida Kogyo (YKK), Murata Manufacturing Co., and TDK. Florida now has 51 Japanese companies, North Carolina 36, Tennessee 23, Virginia 14, South Carolina 10, and Alabama 9 (all as of June 1984).

Governor Lamar Alexander of Tennessee is particularly enthusiastic in this respect, visiting Japan two or three times every year. Following earlier ventures by Toshiba and Matsushita, Nissan Motor Co. and Bridgestone Tire Co. now operate factories in Tennessee, and Komatsu Ltd. has decided to locate a new operation there.

The influence of the aggressive activities of these southeastern conferences has now spread to states in other regions. These successful experiences of the Japan-regional U.S. economic societies in promoting economic exchange over ten or twenty years are now creating great enthusiasm for engaging in economic activities which are well suited to the new social and economic trends. This is a development that warrants careful attention. The Japan-California Society held its 21st convention in Kobe in May 1984. This society will soon be joined by a number of other Western states to form the Japan-California-Western Society, which will then broaden its activities into new areas.

As I have traveled about the United States, I have been impressed with the strong determination of the people in many states to improve their state economies by attracting high-tech industry as well as engaging in businesses which have become traditional to the regions. Silicon Valley — the California center of semiconductor production — has now reached a state of saturation, and is looking for other areas to develop in. At the same time, many states are now actively soliciting advanced American industries as well as looking hopefully to the establishment of local Japanese factories as a means of reinforcing and accelerating the transition to industries that have greater future potential. Such trends are particularly noticeable in Oregon, Washington, and Nevada. In the meantime, new centers of high-tech industry are now developing in the outskirts of both Phoenix, Arizona, and Denver, Colorado.

There is a high-tech area on the outskirts of Boston, Massachusetts, which rivals Silicon Valley, but I think Japanese interests would do well to pay more attention to the enthusiasm in promoting high-tech industries now being shown in the other five New England states of Maine, New Hampshire, Vermont, Rhode Island, and Connecticut.

The movement of Japanese industry into the United States has become very brisk in the past few years. From 1980 to 1983, this Japanese investment grew each year by about $2 billion, reaching a total of $11.15 billion by the end of 1983 to surpass Canada ($11.1 billion), West Germany ($10.4 billion), and rank third behind England ($32.5 billion) and the Netherlands ($28.8 billion).

Broken down by industry, the trading companies and other exporters and importers account for the lion's share of this business

(69%), followed by manufacturing companies (15%) and the financial industry (12%). More recently, however, the trend in setting up new Japanese enterprises in the United States is more toward manufacturing than trading, with ventures in the research-and-development and high-tech fields such as computers, optical communications, and optical disks being particularly conspicuous. These operations include, for example, an LSI plant in Roseville, California, and a communications equipment factory in Hillsboro, Oregon — both owned and operated by Nippon Electric Co. (NEC); Hitachi Ltd's LSI plant in Irving, Texas; Sumitomo Electric Industries' optical fiber factory and research laboratory in Research Triangle Park, North Carolina; Kobe Steel's research laboratory, also located in Research Triangle Park; Kyoto Ceramic's new materials laboratory in Vancouver, Washington; Nippondenso's new materials laboratory (under construction) in Southfield, Michigan; and a new Fujitsu operation in Oregon. There are now some 370 Japan-based manufacturing plants in the United States, and, according to Commerce Under Secretary Olmer, direct Japanese investments in America have resulted in the creation of 150,000 jobs (90,000 in manufacturing alone).

A prominent factor in the rapid development of advanced-technology enterprises in the United States is the cooperation between industry and academia. The foundations of Silicon Valley's prosperity, for example, were created by Stanford University — one of the finest universities in America — in neighboring Palo Alto, and by the University of California, which has campuses at Berkeley, Los Angeles, San Diego, and six other locations throughout the state. On the East Coast, similarly, high-tech industries have grown up in the outskirts of Boston as an outgrowth of research carried on at nearby Harvard University and the Massachusetts Institute of Technology.

In order to nurture and develop new industries, many states devote enormous energy to attracting outstanding researchers to their local universities and to training and retaining more science and engineering students. In Texas, for example, the growth of aerospace and electronics industries based in Houston, Dallas, and the San Antonio-Austin industrial belt is promoted by the University of Texas (Austin campus). This university is well known for its success in attracting Nobel Prize recipients to its faculty. North Carolina has built the world's largest research facility com-

55

plex within what it calls the "Research Triangle" of Raleigh, Durham, and Chapel Hill. This complex is supported by research and development work carried on by the University of North Carolina, Duke University, and North Carolina State University. This co-operation between industry and academia will no doubt continue to be a driving force in promoting and supporting further industrial growth.

The greatest obstacle in attracting industry to the United States from Japan and other foreign countries was the unitary tax problem, as typified in California. Under a unitary tax system, a state applies its tax rates not only to profits earned by a company from operations in that state, but also to the combined profits of the parent company, subsidiaries, and affiliated companies operating in other states or other countries. Even if its local operation is operating in the red, therefore, a company may find itself liable to heavy taxation. A foreign company, moreover, will be subject to double taxation — by its own country and by the state. Accordingly, enthusiasm for investing in a state which has a unitary tax system is quickly cooled. The Japanese government has encouraged the U.S. government to abolish the unitary tax systems. The federal government in Washington seemed very sympathetic toward alleviating these tax burdens, but every state has the sovereign right to impose its own taxes, and the federal government was in no position to force its will in this matter upon the states. Thus Washington could do nothing but wait for each state government to take independent action. It was because of this situation that Treasury Secretary Donald Regan asked our Embassy to challenge the various states on the unfairness of their tax laws. The federal government then held numerous conferences to study the problems of the various unitary tax states. As a result, the states agreed to restructure their tax laws in accordance with the general principle of taxing only income that is from local operations, while Washington promised to cooperate by providing the necessary information.

Partly due to the obvious advantages of geographic accessibility, Japanese commercial operations in the past tended to concentrate in California, but interest in doing business in that state has waned as unitary taxation there has become increasingly onerous. Keenly aware of this problem, in September 1984, Keidanren (Japan Federation of Business Organizations) sent out two tudy groups, headed by Sony chairman Akio Morita and C. Itoh chairman Seiki Tozaki, respectively, to visit California and other states and impress upon state officials that foreign business investment was being obstructed by the unitary tax system.

Not only were some Japanese companies cutting back on new investments in California, but there were even cases of reversing decisions to set up new operations in California in favor of neighboring Oregon, which abolished its unitary tax system in January 1986.

Some states were soliciting foreign business while imposing unitary taxation. This was clearly inconsistent.

As of the end of 1984, twelve states had unitary tax systems in place. These were Alaska, California, Colorado, Florida, Idaho, Indiana, Massachusetts, Montana, New Hampshire, North Dakota, Oregon, and Utah.

Florida, Oregon, and Indiana subsequently took legislative measures to abolish their unitary tax systems, while Massachusetts not only revised its tax laws but took administrative measures to effectively abolish unitary taxation.

These states, however, must then face the serious problem of how to make up for the lost revenues resulting from abolishing the unitary tax. This is the reason California is having a hard time taking the step. There is a strong grassroots anti-taxation movement in California, as symbolized in the famous "Proposition 13," and the state government already has a large fiscal deficit. Thus California is reluctant to abolish the unitary tax and thereby lose an estimated $500 million in tax revenues. There are now indications that California might impose a new precondition to revising their tax code, namely demanding that the U.S. trade deficit with Japan first be rectified.

In Florida, the unitary tax had been adopted in order to support a larger education budget, which fact then posed a major obstacle to its abolition, but Governor Robert Graham was extremely enthusiastic about attracting industry to the state, and the lost unitary tax revenue was made up for by raising sales taxes.

New Mexico also had a unitary tax system, but this was abolished in April 1983, in order to more effectively attract foreign industry.

There is another problem which foreign companies investing directly in the United States must face, namely the perennial problem of labor relations. In general, the rate of unionization is extremely low in the South, and the handling of labor relations in that region presents relatively few problems for company management, due in part to the absence of compulsory union membership requirements. In the eastern and Great Lakes regions, Japanese companies have moved with caution, and, with very few exceptions, no particular problems have arisen thus far. Nevertheless, the United Auto Workers (UAW) and United Steel Workers (USW) demand that Japanese companies allow their employees to join these unions. The adroit handling of union relations will continue to be an important concern of companies operating in these regions.

Cooperation with local community interests is another major consideration. I am very happy to see that Japanese companies earn comparatively high marks in this area by cooperating with local charity activities and donation campaigns, for example, or holding Japanese-style sports tournaments, thereby deepening interpersonal relations and developing good will in the community.

Another difficult problem for Japanese companies operating in the United States is that of securing suitable education for the children of their Japanese staff. Many state governors and government officials have exhibited great sensitivity to this problem, however, and I want here to acknowledge their willingness to help alleviate this dilemma.

Much is made of Japan-U.S. economic friction, and the competitive and confrontational aspects of Japan-U.S. relations tend to get the greatest attention, but Japanese business ventures are most enthusiastically welcomed by all the states. This has enormous significance for improved Japan-U.S. relations as more jobs are created for Americans and as the goods produced by these enterprises are sold not only in U.S. markets but also in third-country markets, thereby boosting U.S. exports. Also not to be overlooked is the enormous contribution that U.S.-based Japanese trading operations are making, not only in Japan-U.S. trade, but also in exporting American manufactured goods and agricultural produce to third-country markets. These Japanese trading companies now handle a volume of American exports that ranks third behind Boeing and General Electric. I cannot overemphasize the importance of this contribution, and I believe there is a need to deepen the public awareness of these areas of Japan-U.S. cooperation.

Direct investment, however, must be a two-way street. As of the end of 1983, total U.S. investment in Japan stood at $8.1 billion. This compares to total Japanese investment in America of $11.1 billion. The gap between these two figures has been expanding since 1981. I am optimistic that American investment will grow more rapidly, however, as Japan liberalizes its financial and capital markets and creates a more receptive environment. IBM, Texas Instruments, and other American corporations are expanding their production activities in Japan, and total production and sales resulting from U.S. capital investment in Japan were up to $43.9 billion dollars in 1984, according to statistics. This figure will undoubtedly continue to rise.

More attention is also being given in Japan in recent years to promoting regional economies, and in 1983 a group of economic experts and prefectural officials from northern Kyushu visited the United States and endeavored to attract U.S. industry to Japan.

An episode that illustrates the benefits of Japanese investment in the United States took place during the vigorous negotiations between Saburo Okita, the Japanese representative, and Rubin Askew, the U.S. representative, concerning a government procurement agreement that concerned Nippon Telegraph & Telephone Public Corporation (NTT) prior to its privatization.

One day, in early September, Askew invited Okita and his party to see a baseball game at Yankee Stadium. When a relief pitcher was driven in from the right-field bullpen in a small automobile, Askew pointed to the car and then to the large stadium clock. "That's a Toyota, and that's a Seiko," he grumbled. "Japanese products are now used even in American sports facilities. But American products cannot penetrate the Japanese markets. That's the problem."

Askew once said to me, on another occasion, "I once went to an electric appliance store to buy a new television. Mindful of my position, I asked to see an American-made set. The salesman said he could show me either a Zenith made in Mexico or a Sony made in the United States, and asked which I would prefer. That put me in a real bind. Zenith is an American company, but the strategy of making things in foreign factories to take advantage of lower wages is strongly condemned by the AFL-CIO and other unions as 'exporting employment.'"

I think that the creation of jobs alone is reason enough for the Americans to welcome direct U.S. investments by Japanese companies.

7

Restrictions and Concerns

During the 1950s and early 1960s, when Japan was pouring all of its energies into postwar reconstruction, Japanese industry had to fight an uphill battle to expand its exports to the United States.

The label "made in Japan" at that time was still synonymous with inexpensive and shoddy merchandise made with cheap labor. This was the era when, to most people, Japan-U.S. trade meant Christmas decorations and one-dollar blouses, and when Japanese industrialists received aid from the United States, including guidance in enhancing productivity and implementing quality control measures — the very things that now make Japanese products so highly competitive. Industrial and labor leaders were constantly seeking new information, and flocked to the United States year after year in that pursuit.

In 1965 Japan achieved a surplus for the first time in its trade with the United States. Up until then, Japan had been urging the United States to redress the trade imbalance. Throughout this period Japan received across-the-board U.S. support in joining IMF and the World Bank (1952), GATT (1955), and the United Nations (1956), and then again in getting out from under the GATT Article 35 provisions (which allowed that certain nations were to be exempted from the most-favored-nation treatment called for under GATT). Buttressed by this support, Japan spared no efforts in its quest to be reinstated into international society, and eventually attained that goal.

Meanwhile, among those given the task of carrying on diplomatic relations with the United States, there was continual talk about how Japan-U.S. relations were complicated by a "communication gap," on the one hand, and by an "attention gap," on the other.

Fully cognizant of the importance of the United States to Japan in every sense, the Japanese government was anxious to promote and maintain very close ties with the United States, making this the pivotal consideration in its foreign policy. The United States, however, enjoyed undisputed world dominance at the time, and Americans still tended then to think of Japan as a very minor participant in world affairs. The United States really did not pay enough attention to Japan, and kept Japan inadequately informed of its policies and other vital information. This is the situation that was referred to then by the terms "communication gap" and "attention gap."

In 1963 the Kennedy administration suddenly implemented the interest equalization tax. This action caught Japan totally by surprise, and threw the government — which considered U.S. capital infusions essential to postwar reconstruction — into a panic. Foreign minister Masayoshi Ohira immediately flew off to Washington. The magnitude of the shock suffered by Japan may be judged from this frenzied episode. In 1964 Japan responded by dispatching a team of economic leaders to America, headed by Yoshizane Iwasa, then president of Fuji Bank, with the intention of developing deeper mutual understanding at the private level. This was one attempt to close the communication gap. One outcome of the Iwasa mission was the formation of the Japan-California Association. The Japan-U.S. Business Council has held annual meetings ever since, and interaction between Japanese and American business leaders has continued without interruption.

It was prior to the flap over the 1963 interest equalization tax, in 1961, that agreement was reached on the formation of the cabinet-level Japan-U.S. Joint Economic Committee, the first meeting of which was held in Japan outside of Tokyo. This was the first international conference held between Japan and the United States in which simultaneous interpreting was used officially, and the competent professionals who now interpret instantly between Japanese and English were not available at this time. The conference itself was part of the effort to improve relations between the two nations following the 1960 riots over the ratification of the Japan-U.S. Security Treaty. The communication and attention gaps still posed major problems, however, which the Japanese were kept continually aware of. This situation unfortunately persisted until the early 1970s.

Then came the first and second "Nixon shocks" in July and August of 1971, followed by the ban on soybean exports to Japan in 1973. The political and economic impact of these events for Japan was enormous. As far as the Japanese were concerned, these multiple shocks happened because the United States paid far too little attention to Japan. Subsequently, however, the Americans seemed to have reconsidered the propriety of U.S. behavior toward Japan, and good-will endeavors on both sides have gradually succeeded in closing the communication gap.

In the aftermath of the so-called Nixon shocks, however, forums were established for carrying on much closer dialogue between the Japanese and U.S. governments. The subjects taken up in this dialogue gradually broadened, and opinions were exchanged on global problems as well as on bilateral problems. It is accurate to say that the breadth and depth of these discussions reached levels that would have been unthinkable in the preceding era of diplomacy.

Despite this development, however, there was much controversy in the early 1970s over what was called the "information gap." Japanese newspapers and television carried an enormous quantity of news concerning America every day, so that the Japanese man or woman in the street became quite knowledgeable about the United States. In stark contrast, the media in America offered little or no coverage of Japanese news, unless it involved some natural calamity such as an unusually violent earthquake or typhoon. When a Japanese dignitary such as the prime minister or foreign minister visited the United States, the Japanese were always very anxious to see whether or not the visit would be reported in American newspapers, and our embassy and consulates went to considerable lengths to promote media coverage of these events. As any fair-minded observer would have concluded, Japanese coverage of news of bilateral interest was far better, both in quality and quantity, while the interest in Japan found among the general U.S. population was very sorely lacking.

This changed in the 1970s, and now the volume of Japan-related information being disseminated into American homes has grown to the point where hardly a day goes by without Japan being mentioned in one of the lead news stories. The content as well as the

63

quantity of this news has changed, with broad coverage now given to domestic Japanese political and economic developments as well as to Japan-U.S. economic relations. It has even become common in America today to see articles and documentaries dealing with Japanese educational problems and other aspects of Japanese society. A much larger number of American journalists now reside in Tokyo, growing from 43 in 1975 to 79 as of this writing (comparing to 47 Japanese journalists now assigned to Washington). The number of stories filed by these foreign journalists has grown prodigiously, and Tokyo is rapidly becoming a major source of political, economic, and other news. The so-called "information gap" has been substantially narrowed.

These developments reflect the fact that Japan is now the second most powerful economic power in the world, after the United States, and the fact that the two nations together account for some 35 percent of world GNP. It has become nonsensical to leave Japan out of any serious consideration of the global economy.

The fact is that Japan, during the late 1970s and into the 1980s, has come to exercise an active role in world politics.

Foreign news editors of the major U.S. dailies all testify to the priority handling that they give, whenever possible, to the stories filed by their reporters in Tokyo. This probably reflects both a response to changing concerns among American readers and a conscious decision in view of changing realities. This is making it all the more crucial that American journalists reporting from Tokyo file the important news stories accurately and quickly, and that they be able to supply the background information necessary for understanding those stories.

But the need extends beyond Tokyo. Now that both U.S. government officials and media representatives are keenly interested in news from Japan, the Japanese Embassy and consulates in the United States must be prepared to respond promptly to requests for factual or background information and even to initiate the dissemination of such information when that is appropriate.

In former times, the Foreign Ministry's contact with foreign journalists in Tokyo was quite limited, and was considered one of the secondary functions of the News Department under the Public Information and Cultural Affairs Bureau (now the Foreign Ministry News Office). This system was replaced with the establishment of the Foreign Press office, which since the recent structural reforms has been upgraded to the International News section. This evolution is in keeping with the changing needs of the times. The conference on public information in the United States that is held annually in Washington by the Foreign Ministry, and participated in by the Embassy and the consulates, is another indication of how keen the Japanese are to carry on public information activities so that both the U.S. government and Americans in general will be provided with accurate information on Japan.

As is frequently emphasized, however, public information activities, in order to be effective, must be based on substance and not just on PR techniques. Public relations without substance, in fact, is a contradiction in terms.

Although the information gap, attention gap, and communication gap have all been greatly narrowed, there remains the pressing need to work even harder on getting down to the real substance of the issues. If indeed these various gaps have now been eliminated or at least measurably improved, then why are stories of intense Japan-U.S. economic friction so much in the news, and why do the diatribes against Japan continue to be heard in the halls of Congress with such regularity?

Part of the answer lies in the persistence of what we may call the "perception gap." There is a world of difference between the way that an American views and understands Japanese economic activity and the way that a Japanese views and understands that same activity. In other words, the portrait of Japan that the American draws in his mind is very unlike the portrait drawn by the Japanese in his mind.

A constant theme in the debates over Japan-U.S. economic friction is that of the closed nature of the Japanese marketplace.

Many of the U.S. officials who engaged in trade negotiations with Japan in the 1970s and early 1980s, and many of the Americans who carried on private business relations with Japan during that period, are fully convinced that American products cannot penetrate the Japanese market because it is closed, and that efforts to invest in Japan are discouraged for the same reason.

Once this perception forms in the mind, it is extremely difficult to dislodge. To make matters worse, Japanese economic and societal developments take place at such a dizzying pace that I believe it is very hard for American officials and businessmen to

65

keep up with the changes. They tend to evaluate the current situation in terms of their former experiences and impressions.

There have no doubt also been a few cases of American company representatives excusing their failure in achieving good business results in Japan by shifting the blame to the closed nature of Japanese markets.

Many funny stories are told about American business representatives in Japan complaining of Tokyo's high prices in reports to their home offices in the United States. There was one story of the local office manager who asked his home office to increase living expenses in view of the high cost of living in Tokyo. The American home office responded with the following directive. "Your living expenses are rising because you people are living in such plush accommodations, with names like 'Chateau X' and 'Palace Y.' Move into more ordinary accommodations." In Japan, names like this are of course not applied to large palatial residences, but rather to newly constructed apartment buildings. To people back in the home office, however, these addresses evoked images of turreted castles and expansive palaces. This story may well be apocryphal, but it nevertheless reflects the tribulations of a foreign manager in Japan.

Quite a number of American companies have undertaken successful operations in Japan, but such companies are loath to divulge to outsiders any feelings of satisfaction they may entertain. When it comes to expressing their dissatisfactions and gripes, however, this they do readily and vociferously. And — never mind what the underlying reasons may be — these protests tend to find sympathetic ears in Congress. Their cummulative effect has resulted in the unshakable conviction all across America that Japanese markets are closed.

The Japanese, meanwhile, have the idea that their markets are wide open. At the conclusion of the so-called Tokyo round in 1988, Japan's fixed tariff rate was 3 percent, lower than both the U.S. rate of 4 percent and the common market rate of 5 percent, and in fact the lowest import duty rate of any of the advanced nations. Also significant is the fact that, with the exception of the remaining import restrictions on such agricultural products as beef and oranges, Japan employs no import restrictions. Hence Japanese markets seem altogether open in our perspective, but that perspective is not shared by our friends abroad.

"They may call them 'residual' import restrictions," say Japan's detractors, "but they are in fact GATT treaty infractions. If the Japanese are unwilling to agree to abolishing these in their trade negotiations with the United States, then an international settlement should be sought, based on the GATT provisions. Unwillingness to cooperate even in this can only mean that Japan does not want to open its markets." Vigorous protest is also voiced against the non-tariff barriers to trade.

This is a clear example of how our respective interpretations of the same phenomena differ in the debate over market access. It must be admitted that such conflicting interpretations constitute a root cause of today's economic frictions.

Another point of conflicting perspective and interpretation is the relative strength of Japan's economy. Americans tend to overestimate that strength, while we Japanese tend to underestimate it. The way the typical Japanese perceives national prosperity today is still more governed by the narrow dimensions of his or her living quarters than by the enormous size of Japan's GNP—a perception that greatly contrasts with the foreigner's image of Japan as a great economic behemoth.

Views on the proper role of government are also conflicting. Americans readily and publicly identify government as an enemy of business. In their eyes, the Japanese government exercises a dominant role in regulating and guiding Japanese industry. This perception then gives rise to charges that Japanese industrial policies in general—and specific industry promotion policies in particular—constitute unfair subsidization of industry by the government. The Japanese see things quite differently. As far as they are concerned, Japan has abolished its regulated-economy approach and liberalized its industrial controls. The government's authority has been sharply curtailed, and the measures to promote certain favored industries are a thing of the past. The government still points the way to future economic expansion, but specific investment plans are determined solely on the basis of the independent economic judgment exercised within each company.

U.S. industrialists see themselves as the ongoing victims of unfair Japanese competition and demand that something be done to alleviate their plight. The Japanese insist that the responsibility for the failing competitiveness of American goods lies in America, pointing out that the demand for superior Japanese goods is strong among U.S. industrial buyers as well as among U.S. consumers. There is nothing unnatural in Japanese industry responding to such demand, say the Japanese.

As the U.S. economy has recovered, American industrialists have regained their former self-confidence, and now exhibit a kind of psychological reaction against their Japanese counterparts who are forever extolling the merits of Japanese management practices—behavior that strikes the Americans as arrogant and as signifying the demise of the old Japanese modesty. The Japanese, for their part, are baffled and indeed incensed by the high-handed demands that the United States keeps making upon Japan, demands that strike them as meddling in Japanese internal affairs.

Further conflict arises in connection with research and development. Americans charge that Japan funnels enormous resources into developing industrial applications, while giving scant attention to basic research, thereby achieving an unfair competitive advantage. The Japanese dismiss this charge as being beside the point, arguing that the development of practical applications is the fundamental objective of industrial enterprise.

In an interview by the *Washington Post* in late March of 1985, Mike Mansfield, U.S. Ambassador to Japan, said that "the Japanese market is not as closed as Americans believe, nor is the U.S. market as open as Americans believe." This statement is right on the mark. We need to go further, however, and admit that the Japanese market is not as open as we Japanese believe. And we must not falter in our efforts to open the doors wider still if we are to change the negative image of Japan that Americans now harbor.

Many Americans insist that America's enormous trade deficit with Japan is due to the fact that Japanese markets are closed. According to an interesting argument recently set forth in this ongoing debate, however, it is impossible—given the extent to which commercial products have now been internationalized—to measure the openness of a market through trade statistics.

In this view, the true situation can only be elevated by looking at the production and sales figures that are generated in a given country by capital invested from other countries and factoring comparisons of these data in the evaluations that are based on export statistics. When this is done Japan doesn't look so bad.

Let us look at this more specifically. In 1984 the total production and sales generated in Japan by U.S. capital was $43.9 billion. When this is added to U.S. exports to Japan in the same year, the total is nearly $70 billion. Meanwhile, direct investment in the United States by Japanese industry has been growing very rapidly over the past two or three years. When this $12.8 billion is added to U.S. imports from Japan for the year, the total is again around $70 billion, so that the two totals roughly balance. The corresponding figures for two years ago were also about the same. In terms of the openness of one country's market to the other, therefore, Japan and the United States have similar circumstances.

When we consider the problems now faced, however, focusing our attention on the sense of victimization and alarm among U.S. industrialists that is at the root of Japan-U.S. economic friction, the argument just presented does not provide quite the right answer.

The U.S. companies that are manufacturing and marketing their products in the Japanese marketplace are primarily such multinational giants as Nippon IBM, NCR, Coca Cola, and Texas Instruments. The American companies in which the sense of victimization and crisis is strongest, however, are the smaller businesses. When we look at the products around which there is constant friction between Japan and the United States — products like motorcycles, machine tools, electronics, or, more recently, plywood and chocolate — we see that it is the smaller American companies that are generating the anti-Japanese sentiment.

Focusing on the foreign activities of the giant multinational corporations in debating market openness may be interesting, not to say unique, but it is doubtful whether this approach will have much effect on the way in which smaller American companies understand the problem. Such companies are spread widely across the United States, and they have influence in Congress.

The behavior of the multinational corporations, moreover, has recently come under vigorous attack in the United States. The AFL-CIO and other powerful labor unions harshly condemn multinational corporations for "exporting jobs" by increasingly basing their production centers abroad in the interest of securing cheap labor. Such developments cast doubt on the viability of any approach to Japan-U.S. trade problems that overemphasizes the role of multinationals.

69

8

Attempts to Relieve
the Tensions

From the time of its basic decision made in December 1981, until April 1985, the Japanese government has made seven announcements concerning its so-called market-opening policies (see appendix 1). This averages out to two policy announcements a year and reflects the fact that more and more initiatives are being taken to open Japan's markets. These aggressive measures are unprecedented in Japan, in terms of both their scale and their speed of implementation. They represent an enduring political resolve on the part of the government, which has pushed through these policies in the face of stiff domestic opposition and promote widespread demand for a more passive approach. Despite these facts, however, American officials have become increasingly suspicious of Japan's trade policies. Each new announcement from Tokyo has been greeted with expressions of exasperation from Congress. Why are the Japanese initiatives received with so little enthusiasm?

And there is another question. Despite the six batteries of market-opening measures implemented by Japan over the three-year period ending in 1984, why has America's trade deficit with Japan doubled in just three years, from $18.0 billion in 1981 to $36.8 billion in 1984? Many Americans are afraid that, at this rate, the trade deficit with Japan will rise well above $40 billion dollars in 1985, and when they look at the steep upward curve being tracked by this deficit they naturally feel compelled to take strong countermeasures. But the biggest single factor of all is the bad impression that Americans have gotten of Japan, i.e., that

Japan only takes action when pressured to do so from abroad, and then only reluctantly, doing the bare minimum necessary to maintain appearances.

One example of this concerns the reconsideration of the so-called standards and certification system. When Japan determined to implement its first market-opening policies in December 1981, U.S. observers were delighted that it called for the standards and certification system to be broadly modified and its required procedures simplified, and believed that far-reaching reforms would be promptly implemented. However, after these modifications and simplifications were again proclaimed in the second and third market-opening policy announcements (May 1982, and January 1983, respectively), Americans began to think that Japan was all talk and no action, and, ironically to the Japanese, American feelings of distrust and suspicion were deepened.

Reinforcing this trend were such irritating matters as the problem over metal baseball bats, which became a symbol that was often alluded to. U.S. metal bat manufacturers complained that their efforts to market these products in Japan were frustrated by an endless series of obstacles. First there were the tests that had to be conducted in complying with the consumer product safety law that was administered by MITI. Domestically produced goods were perfunctorily approved at the local factory, but there was no such system available for imports. This would mean that every single bat would have to be tested, although in practice only random samples had to be tested. These tests took time and increased costs. When the American manufacturers complained that this posed an unfair import obstacle, the U.S. Commerce Department began negotiations to get Japan to change its system. After extended bilateral haggling, MITI concluded that, in enforcing the consumer product safety law, there was no need to test each and every bat. Thinking that the issue was thereby resolved, the Commerce Department expressed its satisfaction. But then another barrier was encountered in connection with the Japan Amateur Sports Association (JASA), which is under the jurisdiction of the Ministry of Education. This problem was resolved through the efforts of concerned officials, however, and the matter was thought to be finally settled. Then it was learned that the by-laws of the Japan High School Baseball Federation required players of member high schools to use only domestically manufactured bats. Thus one obstacle was overcome only to be met with another and yet another, like the problem of how far one must peel an onion before it is really peeled. Feelings of distrust and frustration deepened.

I recall a visit to Secretary of Commerce Malcolm Baldrige's office and being shown a commemorative shield in which was fixed a model metal bat. "The manufacturers presented this to me," explained Baldrige with a wry smile, "as a token of their appreciation for our negotiating with Japan in getting the trade barriers removed. But, in view of subsequent developments, it looks like I'm going to have to send it back to them."

The metal bat flap did get resolved after the High School Baseball Federation revised its by-laws. Unfortunately, however, it left American officials with more deeply rooted feelings of distrust and suspicion. Once such feelings were stirred up, everything Japanese came to be eyed with suspicion. These are the feelings that are brewing beneath the surface and fueling the vociferous protests against Japan voiced in Congress in the context of Japan-U.S. economic friction.

In January 1982, the Japanese government announced the formation of the Office of Trade Ombudsmen (OTO). This office was to play a role in ensuring the reform of the standards and certification system. The concept was unconventional in terms of traditional Japanese administrative organizations. Claims and complaints from overseas would no longer be processed through the red tape of the hierarchical bureaucracy, but would be responded to quickly and conclusively by the OTO.

It was expected that, in conjunction with the reform of the standards and certification system, the OTO would play a big part in overcoming the procedural obstacles to imports. When actual operations got underway, however, American officials began to grumble that their complaints were not adequately dealt with by the OTO and that the replies received from that office did not step beyond conventional restraints. If they went to the OTO with a problem, they said, they themselves became the objects of criticism and harassment from the government office originally handling the matter. Quite a number of such cases of dissatisfaction were brought to the attention of the Reagan administration, and the prevailing view among U.S. officials is that the OTO is a disappointment, having failed in its basic mission.

American officials have recently been expressing great dissatisfaction with Japan's bureaucracy. Following the OECD cabinet-level meeting in Paris, but prior to the Bonn Summit, Foreign Minister Shintaro Abe visited the United States, and Vice President Bush, in a morning conference, reportedly criticized Japan's bureaucratic system. This news was received with dismay in Japan, where people were astonished to think that the critical attitudes of Americans now extended to the very nature of the Japanese government bureaucracy. I think, however, that what Americans mean by the term *bureaucracy* is much more limited than the Japanese concept.

Judging from all the conversations I had during my tour in Washington, I think it accurate to say that George Bush was addressing certain problems that he perceived not in the Japanese bureaucratic system itself but rather in the lower levels of bureaucracy where policies are ultimately enforced.

The effectiveness of the Japanese bureaucracy is widely commended in the United States, especially when compared with the federal bureaucracy in Washington. Americans may look with envy at the administrative efficiency of the Japanese bureaucracy, but they never seriously speak disparagingly of it. What Americans are unhappy about is the multitude of unforeseen discretionary actions that seem to lie in wait for them at the lower bureaucratic levels, ready to impede U.S. export operations at every turn.

In the Japanese government, the prime minister, his cabinet ministers, and the various officials in charge of enforcing government policy are all aware of the pressing need to remove trade barriers, but this resolve has a hard time filtering down to the lowest levels of government, and in some cases it meets with resistance at those levels — a situation that higher-level officials have recently come to recognize.

I think it safe to say that this is the real focus of the criticism leveled at the Japanese bureaucracy in America.

In other words, American business interests (or their representatives in Japan) have come to hold various grievances and frustrations that have spread throughout U.S. industry and come to the attention of members of Congress. Thus an atmosphere has evolved in which the administration in Washington has felt constrained to lodge strong protests against certain practices encountered in the lower levels of the Japanese bureaucracy.

I am reminded of something that happened some time ago, back when Japan and the United States were continually negotiating over the cigarette problem. Both the Ministry of Finance (MOF) and the Japan Monopoly Corporation (the government-directed entity that controlled tobacco business at the time) had explained publicly that imported cigarettes were not handled any differently than cigarettes made in Japan. Not long after this, the Journal of Commerce in the United States printed a piece that was extremely skeptical of the Japanese position. This article by its Tokyo correspondent reported that a local agency of the Monopoly Corporation had distributed an internal directive that advised tobacco retailers to "display domestic cigarette brands prominently, but display imported brands so that they are as inconspicuous as possible." The Public Corporation interceded immediately, of course, seeking to remedy the situation, but the damage had been done. It is extremely difficult to erase an impression once it has been reinforced with media coverage. I think that things of this nature, multiplied over time, have led to the criticism and suspicion that is currently directed against the lower levels of the Japanese bureaucracy.

As part of the move to streamline administrative procedures, studies are now being done on the relaxation or removal of certain regulations. From the standpoint of removing import barriers, and given the momentum of recent new trends, I think we should thoroughly reevaluate all trade restrictions and insure that administrative procedures are clear even down to the clerk or "window" level.

A meeting between the Japanese foreign minister and the U.S. Secretary of State was held on April 30 in Washington, in anticipation of the Bonn Summit to be held in early May. At the meeting, Secretary of State George Shultz urged Foreign Minister Abe to expand Japanese domestic demand. News of this statement resulted in wide debate in Japan over macroeconomic policy.

At the April 30 meeting, according to newspaper reports, Shultz gave Abe the text of a speech that he had given at Princeton University on April 11, and then said the following: "In Japan, the propensity to save is very high. The surplus capital created by those savings is flowing into the United States in the form of securities investments, without being funneled into domestic investment or consumption. This is an undesirable situation, and, to correct it, Japan should endeavor to expand domestic demand." (See appendix 2.)

This statement gave rise to the argument that the narrowly one-dimensional economic policy of fiscal reconstruction (based on the policy course formerly recommended by the Ad Hoc Council on Administrative Reform) was now even being criticized by the United States. Others argued that the high savings rate was a reflection of the Japanese virtue of frugality, something that no one should criticize. Still others were outraged by the United States' criticism of Japan's tight financial policies (which were directed toward fiscal reconstruction), contending that this was indeed meddling in Japan's internal affairs. These debates became quite spirited.

I think, however, that some of this reasoning is somewhat errant. Upon reading Shultz's Princeton speech very carefully, one sees that he is basically saying three things.

Shultz, to begin with, devotes about half of the speech to the urgent necessity for the United States to do everything possible to reduce the enormous federal deficit that is causing the high interest rates and the strong dollar.

He then turns his attention to Europe's economic stagnation and calls for the rationalization of labor relations and the relaxation of structural rigidity.

Finally, he argues that Japan — as a nation responsible for a large percentage of the world economy — should expand domestic demand, and redirect the surplus capital generated by the high savings rate into domestic investment and domestic consumption.

This idea of stimulating Japan's domestic demand was at that time being urged by Paul Volcker, chairman of the Federal Reserve Board. According to this view, one of the causes of the current strong dollar versus weak yen problem is that surplus Japanese capital is flowing into the U.S. market in great quantities, funneled into U.S. Treasury bills and other securities. In order to rectify the situation, therefore, Japan should expand domestic demand and actively encourage both domestic investment and domestic consumption.

When Mr. Shintaro Abe went to New York in September 1983, to attend the UN General Assembly, Mr. George Shultz, a trained economist in his own right, availed himself of the opportunity to meet with the Japanese foreign minister and to bring up the yen-dollar problem.

Some officials in Japan were dubious as to why the Secretary of State should express such keen interest in foreign exchange matters, these ordinarily outside his bailiwick. However, when President Reagan visited Japan that same year, in November, the Americans made a proposal. Subsequently, based on the U.S. proposal, the Special Yen-Dollar Working Subcommittee was jointly formed by the Japanese Financial Ministry and the U.S. Treasury Department. The work of this subcommittee resulted in the publication of a report in May 1984, leaving American officials satisfied that they had achieved their goal of getting Japan to liberalize its financial market and internationalize the yen. In light of this series of events, it is evident that Shultz did not bring up the yen-dollar issue to Abe on a mere whim.

It is in this context, then, in which one should understand both the Princeton speech and the comments made by Shultz to Abe.

In the economic statement issued at the close of the Bonn Summit in May, specific economic measures were emphasized for each of the seven participating nations as ways of maintaining future growth and full employment. The single measure emphasized for the United States was the sharp reduction of its fiscal deficit. For the European nations the priorities were to bring inflation under control and to create more jobs through promoting advanced-technology industries and small businesses. The measures advocated for Japan were to promote investment by making its markets more functional, to internationalize the yen, to open its markets to outsiders, and to increase exports. This Bonn economic statement seems to echo Shultz's speech at Princeton.

Let us look more closely at Japan's investments in foreign securities. Roughly $50 billion flows overseas from Japan every year, of which some $40 billion are said to be directed into U.S. securities. Domestically, the United States issues an enormous volume of Treasury bills every year to finance its enormous fiscal deficit. By purchasing large lots of these bills, Japan is cooperating financially with the U.S. government. Japan should be commended for this behavior, not reprimanded for it. So goes one line of argument.

The real problem, however, is the crisis mentality and the sense of victimization that is so prevalent in Congress and among the industrial and labor leaders who have influence in Congress. The crisis mentality is especially strong in the industrial states that border the Great Lakes. This is reflected in the fact that, at the conference held annually in Washington for Japanese ambassadors and consuls residing in the United States, the strongest anti-Japanese public sentiment is always reported by the consul general from Chicago, the Japanese diplomat responsible for the Great Lakes region.

It is true that the Financial people one meets express approval of deepening financial ties between Japan and the United States and, in that sense, they are not vehemently critical of Japan. This attitude among the financial community, unfortunately, is not at all shared among those in the industrial community. Industrialists are not the least concerned with so-called invisible trade or other macro capital movements; such matters have no place in their interpretation of the problem. Thus the argument that they should not complain about the trade deficit since Japan cooperates by pouring capital into the system falls quite short of the mark.

It may indeed be said that American industrialists are not used to thinking of both movements of physical things and transfers of money as one integrated process. They are only interested directly in whether American-made products get sold or not.

We Japanese, for another thing, have been telling our American friends all along that the trade imbalance is never going to get any better until effective measures are taken to reduce the federal deficit which is causing the high interest rates and strong dollar.

On this point, former Treasury Secretary Donald Regan (currently the president's chief of staff) has expressed his opinion as follows. If high interest rates follow from a large fiscal deficit, then how do you explain the fact that Japan's interest rates are low while it carries a fiscal deficit of 4.6 percent of GNP, which is larger than America's? This tells us, says Regan, that the two factors are not directly related. There are other economists who hold strongly to the opinion that a strong dollar exchange rate is not always the result of high interest rates. Some theorists point to the so-called safe-haven effect, i.e., that capital flows into the United States because the dollar is the safest currency. Accordingly, the world's surplus capital should continue to flow into the United States even if U.S. interest rates were to come down a little, and the dollar would not be easily or necessarily weakened.

Trade Representative William Brock, who became labor secretary, has publicly testified that 70 or 80 percent of the U.S. trade imbalance is due to foreign exchange, while the remaining 20 or 30 percent is due to import barriers set up by America's trading partners. The experts will perhaps argue about the actual proportion, whether it is 8 to 2 or 7 to 3. At any rate, Americans do not believe that the trade deficit can be satisfactorily explained merely in terms of the strong dollar and weak yen.

Senator John Danforth, whom I met just prior to turning over the ambassadorship to my successor, is a prime example. "You say that the strong dollar and weak yen are increasing exports to the United States, and suppressing exports to Japan," said Danforth. "How then does Japan explain the fact that European products cannot penetrate the Japanese market, despite the strong yen and weak pound, the strong yen and weak franc, and the strong yen and weak mark?"

I have already written about C. Fred Bergsten (director of the Institute for International Economics and former assistant secretary of treasury in the Carter administration) who, focusing on the surplus Japanese capital flowing into the United States in the form of securities investments, and the effect of this in weakening the yen, called for restrictions on Japanese capital exports. The Reagan administration, however, having proclaimed itself the champion of free trade, can hardly adopt Bergsten's proposal, which seeks to artificially stop the flow of capital by means of governmental regulation. On the other hand, it is desirable that Japan should actively stimulate investment and consumption at home, and thereby naturally stop the flow into the United States of the surplus capital generated by the high Japanese savings rate. Thus the portion of Shultz's Princeton speech that dealt with Japan should be understood as calling upon Japan to consider economic policy measures that would promote domestic demand.

When an American official makes a statement regarding Japan, we need to ask why he or she made that statement, analyze the broader context in which it was made, and carefully consider the basis for the American point of view. When we fail to do this, our conclusions may create embarrassing situations for ourselves.

Appendix 1

The specific decisions (in summary) of the seven announcements concerning Japanese market-opening measures, as approved by the Economic Cabinet Conference on Economic Countermeasures, were as follows:

FIRST POLICY ANNOUNCEMENT
FOREIGN TRADE POLICY (12/16/81)

I. Market-Opening Measures

1. Revision of Import Testing Procedures (this provision adopted 1/30/82)

A. Of the 99 matters raised by foreign nations, move as rapidly as possible to implement "the 67 matters on which reform measures are to be taken," and, as a general rule, consolidate, by the end of March 1982, the results of studies on "the 9 matters requiring further study."

B. The Administrative Management Agency will perform administrative oversight on the aforesaid 67 matters during fiscal 1982.

C. The Ministry of Foreign Affairs will be responsible for adequately explaining these reform measures to foreign nations, while the appropriate ministries and agencies will explain them to their regional offices and to industrial interest groups.

D. The Office of Trade Ombudsmen (OTO) will be established to handle future complaints.

E. From now on, in carrying out import testing procedures, this will be done fairly and reasonably, giving due consideration to the spirit of market openness.

2. Relaxation of Import Restrictions

Remaining import restrictions will be duly reviewed.

3. Import Duty Reduction

The MTN [Multilateral Trade Negotiation] reductions will be accelerated by two years, across the board, and the import duty on whiskey will be reduced, so that, for 1,653 items, the mean tariff rate will be lowered from 8% to 6.5%. This represents a reduction of approximately 16%.

II. Import Promoting Measures

1. Implementation of Emergency Import Foreign-Currency Lending

This will be implemented as an emergency measure, involving a total of $500 million. The interest rate applied will be the U.S. T-bill rate plus 0.125%.

2. Promotion of Emergency Reserves

A. Increase emergency oil reserves by 150 kiloliters in fiscal 1982,

B. promote stockpiling of rare metals in private sector, and

C. employ foreign grains in providing KR food aid.

3. Sending Import Missions Abroad, Sponsoring Product Exhibitions

III. Export Measures

Base policy on trade expansion and balance; avoid concentrated high-volume exports of specified items.

IV. Industrial Cooperation Measures

Promote industrial cooperation through exchanging capital and technology with the Common Market nations and others, through joint technological research and development, and by cooperating in third-country markets.

V. Economic Cooperation Measures

Fully achieve the mid-term objectives for the government's Official Development Assistance (ODA) program decided on in January 1981.

SECOND POLICY ANNOUNCEMENT
MARKET-OPENING MEASURES (decided 5/28/82)

I. Reform of Import Testing Procedures

1. Carry on active OTO operations; give priority to resolving metal bat and wild rice problems as soon as possible.

2. Smoothly implement measures to simplify and speed up customs procedures for pharmaceutical and food imports.

3. Insure transparency of criteria for industrial standards by having foreign interests participate in the drafting process.

II. Import Duty Reduction

Reduce or eliminate duties on a total of 215 items. The total value of imports of these 215 items in 1981 was 825.1 billion yen.

1. Items on Which Duties Eliminated

Products of Mining & Manufacturing Industries: Lathes and other machine tools, refrigerators, air conditioners and other household appliances, boilers and other heavy electrical equipment, cut diamonds, and lenses, etc., totaling 96 items.

2. Items on Which Duties Reduced

Products of Mining & Manufacturing Industries: Computers, automobile parts, film, tires, skis, cigarette lighters, and fountain pens, etc., totaling 102 items.

Agricultural Products: Turkey meat, biscuits, chocolate, lemons, limes, sweet almonds, etc., totaling 17 items.

III. Relaxation of Import Restrictions

Among items on which import restrictions remain, expand quotas on herring, processed pork products, canned pineapple, and high-test molasses, and establish minimum import quotas.

IV. Import Expansion

1. Imported Cigarettes: By 1985, all retailers desiring to do so shall be able to handle these products, and during fiscal 1982 and 1983, the 20,000 stores currently handling them will be increased to 70,000 stores. The amounts allowed under the voluntary restrictions on advertising expenses will be increased.

2. Promote implementation of emergency import foreign-currency lending.

3. Promote closer bilateral coordination concerning the pro-

81

motion of Japanese imports of oil from Alaska and coal from western United States.

V. Reforms in Distribution System and Traditional Business Practices

1. Invite opinions from foreign interests to be aired at Trade Conference (Conference on Measures to Promote Manufactured Imports).

2. Create an individual transaction consulting system, employing business consultants.

3. Employ Japan-U.S. Trade Facilitation Committee (TFC) to review products for which improved market access is demanded. Promote meetings between domestic and foreign private companies on soda ash, etc.

4. Intensify oversight in area of distribution of imported goods; strictly enforce antitrust law.

VI. Liberalization of Service Trade

1. Contribute to creation of international rules for service trade within GATT.

2. Strictly maintain national treatment [with respect to foreign parties] in the banking, insurance, and securities industries.

3. Establish window services in appropriate trade organizations for providing information to foreign interests wishing to conduct banking, insurance, or securities operations in Japan.

4. Take measures to more openly welcome direct foreign investment in Japan and to further facilitate capital procurement by foreign nations in the Japanese financial market.

5. Maintain national treatment and relax regulations in data communications area.

6. Promote negotiations between the Japan Federation of Bar Associations and the U.S. National Bar Association concerning foreign attorney activities in Japan.

VII. Advanced Technology

1. Maintain free trade as the basic policy. Promote international cooperation in research and development. Do not discriminate against foreign-financed companies wishing to participate in government-subsidized projects.

2. Study feasibility of multination joint research and joint technological development.

VIII. Other
Review national policies on government procurement, food subsidies, industrial cooperation, export measures, economic cooperation measures, and overseas exchange activities.

* * *   * * *

REMARKS OF PRIME MINISTER
ON ADOPTION MEASURES (Synopsis)

1. In order for these reforms at the system level to produce real results, it is essential that people in both the government and the private sectors adopt—in the actual administration of these policies and in the arena of economic activity—a welcoming attitude toward the influx of foreign goods and foreign capital.

2. Given the context of today's global economic trends, it is most important that Japan act appropriately to its international position in using its national resources to promote the world economy and expand world trade. In that regard, I appeal to all Japanese citizens for their understanding and cooperation.

THIRD POLICY ANNOUNCEMENT
PROMOTION OF IMMEDIATE FOREIGN
ECONOMIC MEASURES (decided 1/13/83)

I. Import Duty Reduction
Reduce or eliminate import duties beginning in fiscal 1983. This will involve 323 items, including those designated in the second policy announcement.

II. Relaxation of Import Restrictions
Beans, peanuts, fruit purees and pastes, non-citrus fruit juices, tomato juice, and tomato catsup sauce

III. Reform of Import Testing Procedures

1. Sponsoring OTO Advisory Conference
Respond to inquiries concerning all OTO activities; support OTO activities.

2. Upgrading OTO Functions

A. Adopt petition-by-agent system.

B. Upgrade contact and coordination functions.

C. Improve resources and procedures for processing complaints.

D. Upgrade regional coordinating conferences.

E. Optimize public relations and coordination activities.

3. Reform of Standards and Certification System; Formation of Contact and Coordination Center.

Complete comprehensive studies, including legal reform, from the perspective of market openness.

4. Further Reform of Import Testing Procedures

Expand list of allowed cosmetic ingredients. Allow foreign companies to put the S mark on their metal bats, accept foreign testing data on electrical goods, etc. — 16 items total.

5. Appropriate Cabinet-Level Measures

Among other things, provide opportunities for cabinet-level opinions to be exchanged with foreign embassies in Japan.

6. Enhancement of Administrative Oversight

IV. Import Promotion

1. Further Promotion of Foreign Cigarette Distribution

A. Increasing Number of Stores Handling Foreign Cigarettes

(i) Extend to retail cigarette outlets in major metropolitan centers (excluding the Tokyo and Osaka regions) throughout Japan by the end of March 1983.

(ii) Extend to retail cigarette outlets in Tokyo and Osaka regions by the end of October 1983.

(iii) Extension to all remaining regions is scheduled to be implemented by the end of 1985, but endeavor to move this schedule up to the end of 1984 for some areas.

B. Imported Cigarette Distribution System

In the future, when dealing with the problems of reforming the Monopoly Corporation, reconsider the distribution system and review the handling procedures under the fiscal revenue system.

2. Expansion of Imports of Finished Goods

A. Make necessary reforms in distribution system and traditional business practices.

B. Develop an even more active business consultant system.

V. Other

1. Export Measures

Avoid concentrated high-volume exports.

2. Industrial Cooperation

Actively promote capital exchange, technological exchange, and cooperation in third-country markets.

3. Procurement by Government-Related Organizations

Continue to faithfully enforce non-discriminatory and competitive procurement procedures within Nippon Telegraph & Telephone Corporation (NTT), and continue to actively implement measures for promoting participation by foreign companies [in the bidding process].

FOURTH ANNOUNCEMENT
GENERAL ECONOMIC MEASURES (10/21/83)

I. Economic Recovery Through Expanded Domestic Demand

1. Promotion of Public Investment

2. Reduction of Income Taxes and Resident Tax

3. Promotion of Private Participation in Public Works Field

4. Promotion of Private Sector Investment

5. Dynamic Implementation of Monetary Policy

II. Market Openness

1. Import Duty Reduction: Conduct studies with a view to implementing the accelerated measures agreed upon in the Tokyo Round beginning in fiscal 1984, excluding agricultural, forestry, and marine products.

2. Broadening of Overall Preferential-Treatment Ceiling Guidelines for Mining and Manufacturing Products: Increase by approximately 50% over fiscal 1983 levels, beginning in fiscal 1984.

3. Reduce or eliminate import duties on 44 separate items.

4. Relaxation of Import Restrictions: Study measures needed, giving consideration to results of consultations with foreign nations.

5. Carry out thoroughgoing reform of the standards and certification system.

6. Active Promotion of OTO Activity: Promote more aggressive action by OTO advisory conference; upgrade foreign public relations activities.

III. Import Promotion

1. Promoting Imports Through Export-Import Bank: Provide low-interest loans for imports of finished goods; improve the system to better facilitate import financing; provide capital loans for improving the program to promote sales of imported goods.

2. Streamline the procedures for obtaining yen-denominated short-term import financing.

3. Upgrade the import-promoting functions of the Japan External Trade Organization (JETRO).

4. Promoting Government Procurement of Imported Goods: Implement government procurement agreements more thoroughly; draw attention in these agreements to regional public organizations.

5. Improving Imported-Goods Distribution Functions: Provide information on Japan's distribution system; actively study ways to make the distribution system for imported goods more effective.

6. Other: Establish a finished-goods import promotion month; send Japanese market-access missions abroad; promote activities of the Import Promotion Committee of the Japan Traders Association; promote activities of Manufactured Goods Importers Association; encourage exporting companies to work at promoting imports; reform distribution system for imported cigarettes.

IV. Capital Influx Promotion

1. Issue government-backed international bonds in the U.S. market.

2. Reform the legal system concerning foreign-currency-denominated government bonds.

V. Promotion of Yen-Denominated International Transactions; Improvement of Capital Market Environment

1. Review of Actual Demand Principle

2. Feasibility Study on Yen-Denominated Trade-Related Bank Acceptances

3. Foreign Company Participation in Financial Fields

VI. Promotion of International Cooperation

1. Promotion of Industrial Cooperation

2. Promotion of Economic Cooperation

3. Cooperation in Funding International Financial Organizations

4. Insuring Reasonable Exports

FIFTH POLICY ANNOUNCEMENT
FOREIGN ECONOMIC MEASURES (4/27/84)

I. Market Openness and Import Promotion
  1. Import Duty Reduction
  A. Reduction or Elimination of Import Duties on Individual Items: 36 agricultural items and 31 mining and manufacturing items—totaling 67 items (United States: colored photographic paper, agricultural machines, pork, down; Canada: magnesium ingots; Europe: mink furs, cock valves, personal accessories; Australia: beef organs, tongue, prepared meat products, electronic measuring instruments, etc.)

On May 16, 3 paper product items and 4 wine items were additionally decided on. When these are included, the list comprises 42 agricultural items and 34 mining and manufacturing items, for a total of 76 items.

  B. Acceleration of Tariff Reduction Measures Agreed Upon in Tokyo Round (2 years earlier for mining and manufacturing goods, 1 year earlier for agricultural, forestry, and marine products)

  C. Expanding and Adding to List of Tax-Free Items Based on Agreement on Civilian Aircraft Trade

  2. Relaxation of Import Restrictions
  A. Beef, oranges, orange juice, grapefruit juice
  B. Other
     (i) Import Liberalization: prepared pork products, high-test molasses, fruit pulp, tropical juices, etc.
     (ii) Expanded Import Quotas: beans, peanuts, corned beef, prepared pineapple products, non-citrus fruit juices, etc.

  3. Liberalization of Imports of Manufactured Tobacco Products and Distribution Reforms

  4. Reform of Standards and Certification System
  A. Active Utilization of Foreign Testing Periods
  B. Acceptance of Foreign Testing Data; Internationalization of Standards and Criteria
  C. Simplifying and Speeding Up Certification Procedures

D. Promotion of Finished-Goods Imports

(i) Implement program to promote market penetration of designated foreign products.

(ii) Support exhibitions of foreign products.

II. Market Openness in Advanced Technological Fields

1. Communications Satellites

A. Purchase by Private Companies of Foreign Communication Satellites

B. Purchase of Communication Satellites by Nippon Telegraph & Telephone Corporation when Denationalized; Purchase by Government

2. Telecommunications Business

3. Software Protection

III. Promotion of Money and Capital Market Liberalization, Yen Internationalization

IV. Promotion of Investment Exchange

1. Operating a Program for Providing Information

2. Operating a Program for Handling Complaints

3. Supporting Investment-Promotion Missions

4. Revising Procedures for Investing in Japan

V. Energy

VI. Domestic Activity of Foreign Attorneys

SIXTH POLICY ANNOUNCEMENT
FOREIGN ECONOMIC MEASURES (12/14/84)

I. Reduction or Elimination of Import Duties

1. Acceleration of Tariff Reduction Measures Agreed Upon in Tokyo Round

For certain designated items, agreement was reached in the Tokyo Round to reduce import duties in stages over an 8-year period, from 1980 to 1987.

A. For the agricultural, forestry, and marine products among the said designated items, accelerate implementation 2 years for items involving developing countries and 1 year for the other items.

B. For the mining and manufacturing products among the said designated items, accelerate implementation 2 years.

2. Elimination of Import Duties on Individual Items

Abolish import duties on some items involving developing countries, in fiscal 1985.

II. Reform of Preferential Customs System

1. Expansion of Preferential-Treatment Ceiling Guidelines

Continuing in fiscal 1985 from 1984, expand the preferential-treatment ceiling guidelines on mining and manufacturing goods by ¥ 100 billion or so (approximately 8%).

2. Reducing Selected Product (SP) List

Remove certain mining and manufacturing items from the SP list (of items on which the tariff rate applied is half the preferential tariff rate).

3. Reducing List of Items Excepted From Special Preferential Measures for Developing Countries

For woven jute products made in undeveloped or developing countries, abolish the preferential-treatment ceiling guidelines and apply special preferential measures.

SEVENTH POLICY ANNOUNCEMENT
FOREIGN ECONOMIC MEASURES (4/9/85)

I. Response to Report of Advisory Committee on Foreign Economic Problems

1. The committee report recommended medium-term government policies, calling specifically for further improving market accessibility, steady growth centered on domestic demand, more investment and industrial cooperation, and responsiveness to developing countries. The government will give every due consideration to these recommendations as it carries out government policy in the future.

2. In order to implement the recommended improvement in market accessibility, the following basic policies concerning an action program will be established and followed.

A. Based on the committee report, an action program will be established, and follow-up monitoring activity will be performed.

B. The action program will be carried on basically for no more than three years. The framework will be drawn up this July.

C. Attention will be given to the opinions of both Japanese and foreign experts, and every effort will be made to achieve transparency.

II. Immediate Measures & Policy Program
1. Improved Market Access & Import Promotion
  A. Import Duty Reduction

(i) Although Japan's import duties are already at a lower level than those of other countries, as of this April 1, the tariff reductions announced last year for individual items will be implemented, together with measures for reforming the preferential customs system. From March 1, moreover, duties on semiconductors will be mutually eliminated by Japan and the United States, based on an agreement between the two nations.

(ii) In order to revitalize the forestry industry, fiscal monetary measures will be implemented, initially for a 5-year period, focusing on (1) promoting increased lumber demand, (2) improving the internal structure of the lumber industry, and (3) emphasizing forest thinning and tree nurturing operations. The progress of this program will be monitored, and, after the third year, positive efforts will be made toward reducing import duties on plywood made from conifer and/or broadleaf wood.

(iii) Tariffs will be lowered on other individual items during the first half of this year.

B. Standards and Certification, Import Testing Procedure Reforms

(i) Reviews will continue to be made on how well the decisions made on March 26, 1983, by the Contact and Coordination Center concerning the standards and certification system are being implemented, and improvements will be sought.

(ii) In the interest of accepting foreign clinical test data on medical equipment and external diagnostic drugs which do not involve racial differences, and of insuring the transparency of the examination and approval process, the Central Drug Commission will provide opportunities for companies seeking product approval, including foreign companies, to listen directly to directive particulars, and to make explanations.

(iii) In addition to recognizing the passage of tall containers under certain conditions, further improvements will be sought in the procedures relating to standards and certification and to testing imported products.

C. Promoting Imports of Finished Goods

(i) Seek cooperation from related companies on imports of finished goods.

(ii) Sponsor and support import fairs.

(iii) Undertake projects to promote sales of certain foreign finished goods.

(iv) Provide increased financing for imports of finished goods.

(v) Conduct campaigns to promote imports.

2. Improving Market Access in Advanced Technological Fields

A. Telecommunications

(i) Continue current policies on Nippon Telegraph & Telephone Corporation materials procurement until December 31, 1986, i.e. through the effective period jointly agreed upon by Japan and the United States. Continue to work toward increased participation by foreign companies in this procurement process.

(ii) Foreign capital controls will not be imposed on type-2 telecommunications business, nor will domestic/foreign discrimination be practiced in this field. The registration and reporting procedures will be made simple and transparent.

As previously, no registration or reporting requirements will be made on data processing operations that employ telecommunications lines.

(iii) Provisions will be made in the accounting regulations to insure fair competition in the telecommunications business.

(iv) The procedures concerning standards and certification for telecommunications terminal equipment will be further simplified, with emphasis placed on preventing future network damage. Foreign data will be accepted and documentation examined by an independent verifying agency that is fair and neutral.

(v) Transparency will be insured.

(vi) Export-Import Bank import financing for companies purchasing communications satellites has been recognized, and action will be taken as early as possible on frequency allocation.

B. Electronics

(i) The cabinet will approve proposed legislation to protect semiconductor chip rights and proposed revisions in the copyright law to protect computer software rights, and efforts will be made to secure Diet passage of these bills during this session.

(ii) Consultations will be conducted with the United States and other advanced nations to gain support in the electronics field for the idea of mutually abolishing semiconductor-related tariffs, as Japan and the United States decided to do, effective March 1.

3. Promotion of Money and Capital Market Liberalization, Yen Internationalization

A. Take measures to permit foreign banks to deal in government bonds, relax the restrictions on Euroyen CD's, and publicize the criteria that foreign banks must meet in order to participate in trust operations.

B. Introduce MMC's, relax the conditions which must be met in issuing CD's, and allow greater flexibility both in issuing Euroyen bonds and making Euroyen loans, and in issuing yen-denominated international bonds.

C. Initiate concrete measures to create a yen-denominated banker's acceptance market and a futures market.

D. Steadily move forward with financial liberalization and the internationalization of the yen, giving due consideration to the report of the Japan-U.S. Yen-Dollar Committee working group.

4. Insuring Reasonable Exports

5. Expansion of Economic Cooperation

Establish new medium-term goals for 1986 and beyond, and work to achieve as much improvement as possible, especially in terms of quality.

6. Promotion of Investment Exchange

A. Beginning in fiscal 1985, set up a new program within the Japan External Trade Organization (JETRO) for conducting special industrial-cooperation consultation operations.

B. Provide active support to regional public organizations in soliciting direct investment in Japan by foreign companies.

7. Domestic Activity of Foreign Attorneys

On March 15, a policy decision was made by the Japan Federation of Bar Associations to recognize the acceptance of foreign attorneys, based upon the principle of substantive reciprocity, and with the prior understanding that foreign attorneys will abide by the voluntary rules of the Federation. The government should now exchange opinions with the Federation and endeavor to achieve a satisfactory resolution of the problem.

* * *   * * *

REMARKS OF PRIME MINISTER (Synopsis)

1. The Japanese government will seek to expand and balance international trade by working toward future economic growth keyed to increased domestic demand and by promoting even greater access to Japanese markets and more active import operations. In particular, we must work toward simplifying many of our domestic systems, making them more transparent and eliminating domestic/foreign discrimination, while continually reevaluating internal market restrictions. Japan is obliged to play a leadership role in the international economic system and must strive to reform its internal systems in accordance with that greater role.

When domestic problems arise during the course of these endeavors, those too must be aggressively tackled, with the basic understanding that free-trade mechanisms — which constitute the foundation of our economy — cannot be preserved or strengthened without shouldering certain costs as well as responsibilities. It is from this position that we will work toward the next new round of GATT negotiations.

2. For many years now, in the postwar era, we have made export growth the focus of our foreign economic policy. Export growth, however, is only one means for achieving greater prosperity for our people. Another means for doing so is to promote import growth, which will give consumers a wider selection.

In the interest of a more prosperous life, I appeal to the Japanese people to be much more receptive to purchasing foreign products. I hope also that the industrial community will do its utmost to expand imports of finished goods.

Japan will not fail to fulfill the roles and the obligations that its economic power mandates. It is our ardent hope that the international community will not succumb to the temptations of protectionist policies but will rather hold resolutely to the course that leads to greater stability and prosperity for all.

Appendix 2

On April 11, 1985, Secretary of State George Shultz made a speech at Princeton University entitled "National Policies and World Prosperity." The portion in which Shultz touched on Japan's high savings rate is excerpted below (from a provisional translation by the Foreign Ministry).

Japan is a special case. It is common knowledge that our $37 billion trade deficit with Japan is causing intense friction between the two nations, and is largely responsible for the recent surge of protectionist sentiment in America. As a measure of Japan's foreign trade imbalance, however, rather than looking at the Japan-U.S. imbalance, it is more instructive to look at Japan's trade surplus with the rest of the world, which has been estimated at $44 billion for 1984.

Japan should be able to reduce this world trade deficit by following policies that would offset the influence of its high savings rate.

Japan's gross private-sector investment exceeds 30% of its GNP, a rate that is roughly 50% higher than the average for other OECD nations. This high saving rate translates into low personal consumption. That portion of production that exceeds private and public consumption is not being used completely for domestic investment. Consequently, the surplus appears in the form of net exports. To put it another way, Japan is now dependent on this large export surplus in maintaining full employment (of its resources).

One possible way of utilizing these resources and reducing the pressure to export would be to open up the opportunities for investment in Japan. For Japan, the resolve to do this is more difficult politically than it is economically. The structural rigidities in the Japanese economy even limit the access available to Japanese companies and investors. If the Japanese government would raise investment incentives and relax the regulative controls that currently obstruct investment by domestic and foreign countries in Japan, all nations, but especially Japan's neighbors, would benefit. Measures are already being taken to liberalize Japan's capital market, in the interest both of utilizing Japanese savings funds more effectively at home and abroad and of broadening the scope of financing choices available to Japanese companies. As these measures are advanced, and the international role of the yen expands, we may expect the value of the yen to more fully reflect the strength of the Japanese economy. In the area of foreign trade, eliminating the barriers to marketing foreign financial services to the Japanese should result in increased market opportunities for foreign vendors, and in increased imports by Japan. The recent statements by Prime Minister Nakasone and the series of measures initiated by the Japanese government to lower trade barriers and promote imports represent an encouraging beginning, which we should applaud. All of these (trade) measures will help to reduce protectionist pressures in other countries as well. In order to correct its chronic trade imbalance, however, Japan must deal first with the imbalance between its savings and investments.

9

American Defense
Policies and Japan

Nearly every year, the director of the Japanese Defense Agency, as well as the chairman and other members of the Joint Staff Council, pay a visit to Washington at the invitation of the U.S. Secretary of Defense and the chairman and other members of the Joint Chiefs of Staff.

In more recent years, as if in response to the visit of the Defense Agency Director General to the United States, visits to Japan by the U.S. Secretary of Defense have become more frequent. The gradual intensification of Japan-U.S. defense cooperation through these exchanges between Japanese and U.S. defense leaders is extremely significant.

Ambassador Mike Mansfield has called Japan-U.S. relations the most important bilateral relationship in the world, and this point of view has come to be widely accepted in the United States. President Reagan himself stressed the importance of this relationship during his visit to Japan in November 1983, declaring that Japan-U.S. relations contributed greatly to world peace and prosperity. The defense policy of the Reagan administration, moreover, recognizes the crucial importance of Asia and the Pacific Ocean in which perspective Japan occupies a central position. This is surely another factor involved in the deepening of ties between the two nations.

Throughout the 1970s, the Japanese government increased the defense budget annually an average of 15 percent, although this rate declined to about 7 percent in the 1980s.

In the latter half of the 1970s, the Soviet Union greatly increased its military presence in the Pacific. In 1978 the Soviets deployed a full division in the "four northern islands" (Kunashiri, Etorofu, Shikotan, and Habomai Islands), and have been gradually building up these forces ever since. In 1979 the Soviet Union invaded Afghanistan, and the armed Vietnamese intrusion into Cambodia was conducted with Soviet backing.

As the military situation in Asia has become increasingly volatile an increasing number of influential Americans have come to hold that Japan must be persuaded to take on a significantly greater defense role.

The Carter administration, and particularly the Defense Department Under Secretary Harold Brown, appealed to the Japanese authorities to "steadily and significantly" build up their defense forces, and at one point there were those who demanded that Japan increase its defense budget by more than 10 percent over the previous year.

In response to this, the Japanese maintained that it was all but impossible to do more than make "steady efforts" in this regard, due to fiscal limitations, national public opinion, and relations with neighboring countries. The Carter administration held undisguised dissatisfaction with this position.

Once the Reagan administration took over the reins of government, however, and Caspar Weinberger was appointed Secretary of Defense, the Americans abandoned the approach of pressuring Japan to increase its defense budget in specific numerical terms. Instead, the Reagan administration pursued a course of quiet diplomacy. Japan was expected to take the initiative in determining its proper role and mission in the world, and based on that determination and self-awareness, to steadily increase its defense expenditures. While carrying on intimate bilateral talks, the new administration in Washington would wait see what steps the Japanese took on their own.

This change in the American posture toward the Japanese defense problem became very apparent in talks that were held in March 1981, when Foreign Minister Masayoshi Ito visited the United States, and again the following June during the U.S. visit of Defense Agency Director General Joji Omura.

When Prime Minister Zenko Suzuki visited the U.S. capital in May of the same year, the joint statement made by the two leaders referred to Japan-U.S. relations as an alliance. The first paragraph of that statement contains the following passage. "The Prime

Minister and the President recognize that the alliance between Japan and the United States is built upon the commonly held values of democracy and freedom, and have reconfirmed the solidarity, friendship, and mutual trust that exists between our two nations."

In Japan, much debate ensued over the meaning of the term "alliance." The Americans, meanwhile, made much of Suzuki's words, reflected in paragraph eight of the joint statement, to the effect that "work must be done to see that even greater efforts are made in order that Japan, autonomously and in keeping with its constitution and basic national policies, upgrade its defense posture in the Japan region and in neighboring sea and air areas, and that the financial burdens on U.S. forces stationed in Japan be further reduced." American officials were most appreciative of remarks made by the prime minister at a press conference following the May summit meeting, in which specific mention was made of a sea-lane defense policy. "The United States has shifted its seventh fleet into the Indian Ocean and Persian Gulf to maintain the security of those regions," said Suzuki. "This unavoidable action has left the seas adjacent to Japan untended. It is proper that Japan should at least defend the ocean regions that are in its own backyard, so to speak. Japan is now pursuing a policy of strengthening its defense forces, within the scope of national self-defense, and in keeping with its constitution. This policy pertains specifically to the seas around Japan, out to a distance of several hundred miles, and to the sea lanes, out to a distance of about 1,000 miles." Since that time, the Reagan administration has maintained a consistent attitude of expecting Japan to play a greater defense role.

In Congress, meanwhile, and particularly in the Senate and House Armed Services committees, it was frequently argued that Japan should be urged to maintain much stronger defense forces. One member of Congress declared that "Japan should be made to pay 2 percent of its GNP as a security-maintenance tax." Another member said that "Japan should have to pay the expenses for operating the U.S. fleet which is now deployed in maintaining the security of the oil trade routes in the Persian Gulf, because the biggest beneficiary of those operations is Japan." Yet another member of Congress opined that "Japan ought to build aircraft carriers and donate them to the United States Navy."

All of these arguments are based on the view that, given the changing international realities, it is unfair for America to shoulder the burgeoning defense costs by itself, and that allied nations should be obliged to foot their end of the bill.

It was against this background that a bill was passed requiring the Defense Department to perform an annual survey to determine how much America's allies were spending on defense, and to report the results to Congress. This bill was sponsored by Senator Carl Levin (Democrat, Michigan), a powerful member of the Senate Armed Services Committee.

Beginning in 1981, the Defense Department has been submitting to Congress every year, at the end of March, a document entitled "Report on Levels of Contribution to Joint Defense by Allied Nations." The subjects of this report are 16 nations comprising Japan and the member nations of NATO (North Atlantic Treaty Organization). The report submitted in March 1985 was made available to the public on May 9.

According to the reports submitted so far, Japan has been ranked 14th or 15th when compard with the NATO nations, and in most of the surveyed categories comes in either last or next to last. In the 1985 report, specific mention is made of the problem of Japan's combat sustainability.

The United States is always concerned with whether or not its international partners are doing their fair share. This is true in the area of economics as well as with regard to defense responsibilities. I think that it behooves us to give careful attention to this American concept of "fairness," and to what it signifies.

Since 1980, Japan's defense budget has grown at an average rate of about 7 percent annually, rising 6.9 percent in fiscal 1985 over the previous year. The growth in the overall national budget was held down to 3.7 percent in 1985, in the interest of fiscal recovery. Despite this stringency, however, high priority was given to increased defense allocations, which grew at the second fastest rate, second only to the 7.9 percent growth in expenditures for economic cooperation. The U.S. government has acknowledged these good-faith efforts by Japan in the defense field, and expects even greater efforts in the future. Nevertheless, from a purely military point of view, the position of the Reagan administration is that the national defense budget must not be determined primarily by fiscal considerations, but rather upon the question of how possible external threats will have to be dealt with. This position was articulated clearly by Secretary of Defense Weinberger in testimony given before Congress. It is evident that the administration — fully aware of the limitations with which the Japanese government is beset — simply wants the Japanese to make reasonable defense efforts that correspond to changing international realities. It is this fundamental global perspective that invites America's strong expectations for sea-lane defense and its keen interest in how the Defense Planning Guidelines adopted in 1976 are being implemented.

As part of the ongoing consultations between Japanese and American defense chiefs, Defense Agency Director General Koichi Kato visited Washington in mid-June, and held a series of meetings with Secretary of Defense Weinberger, Secretary of State Shultz, National Security Advisor Robert McFarlane and importantly placed members of Congress. Through these discussions, Kato sought greater understanding by the Americans of the serious efforts being made by the Japanese government in the defense field. These meetings were very important to the cause of continued defense cooperation.

At the conclusion of Kato's talks in Washington, on June 12, the Senate passed, by a vote of 88 to 7, a measure that called upon Japan to make greater defense efforts. This measure was jointly sponsored by Senators Robert Byrd (Senate Minority Leader, Democrat, West Virginia), Carl Levin (Democrat, Michigan), Lloyd Bentsen (Democrat, Texas), John Kerry, (Democrat, Massachusetts), David Boren (Democrat, Oklahoma), and Strom Thurmond (Republican, South Carolina). The measure — timed to coincide with Kato's visit to Washington — was introduced very suddenly and put to a vote, without any prior consultation with the State Department or Defense Department.

The measure was proposed as an amendment to the Defense Department budget authorization bill. Its provisions included the following:

> It is the consensus of Congress that Japan be called upon (1) to reconsider the Defense Planning Guidelines, (2) to draft 1984 medium-term estimates for achieving sea-lane defense capabilities, and (3) to markedly increase the funding of support for the U.S. military forces stationed in Japan.
>
> The President is required to submit an annual report on the estimated costs of achieving sea-lane defense capabilities,

the degree to which such capabilities have been realized, and the persuasive measures which have been taken with respect to the Japanese government.

This congressional action is diametrically opposed to the posture that the Reagan administration has consistently maintained, namely that of seeking autonomous defense initiatives by the Japanese through quiet diplomacy.

Not long before this amendment was proposed, a member of Senator Levin's staff who strongly advocated the policy of sharing the defense burden among America's allies moved to the Senate Democratic Policy Committee. It is rumored that this individual influenced Minority Leader Byrd's opinion on the subject, resulting in the latter's support of the amendment.

It is interesting to note that Senators Barry Goldwater (chairman of Armed Services Committee, Republican, Arizona), Paul Laxalt (Republican, Nevada), Spark Matsunaga (Democrat, Hawaii), and Bill Bradley (Democrat, New Jersey) were among the seven who voted against the measure. The five Senators absent for the vote included Daniel Inouye (Democrat, Hawaii), Bob Packwood (Republican, Oregon), and John Danforth (Republican, Missouri). Packwood and Danforth were well known for their strong stances against Japan with regard to trade issues. They may have wanted to allay suspicions of a connection between their positions on economic friction and defense.

Not only did this controversial measure contain some very crudely worded provisions, but there were influential Senators who complained later that the procedure was improperly handled, both in the timing of its introduction and in the manner in which it was pushed through.

The idea that each of the allied nations should be called upon to shoulder a fair share of its defense responsibilities is strongly entrenched in Congress. The Byrd amendment, however, carried with it a political attitude that is aimed specifically at Japan, demanding strong and aggressive measures by the Japanese in taking on that fair share in the political, defense, and economic spheres. I think that the episode described above may be rightly understood as an extension to the defense sphere of the demand for fair burden-sharing that has long been made in connection with economic friction.

(In subsequent related developments, the Gejdenson amendment—which also alludes to Japan's defense efforts—was proposed in the House of Representatives for attachment to the foreign aid budget authorization bill, and other interesting episodes unfolded too. But, in the end, a joint session of Congress deleted the demands on Japan to reconsider its Defense Planning Guidelines and to increase its outlays in support of U.S. military forces in Japan. Thus the language of the final Defense Department Budget Authorization Act was considerably toned down from that of the Byrd amendment.)

In the area of Japan-U.S. defense cooperation, Japan makes budgeted outlays of more than $1 billion a year toward maintaining U.S. forces on its soil. Secretary of Defense Weinberger specifically emphasized the crucial significance of this Japanese contribution in the 1986 National Defense Report which he submitted to Congress in February.

One issue that American officials make strong requests for Japanese government cooperation with U.S. military operations in Japan is the night landing practice (NLP) which is conducted over populated Japanese areas by U.S. carrier-based aircraft.

Strong protests have been made by local residents against the jet aircraft noises made near Atsugi Naval Air Station. The United States Navy has continued to show great concern about this issue, contending that maintaining the skills of carrier-aircraft personnel is a critical matter, and that NLP is also extremely important in terms of maintaining the deterrent power of U.S. forces. At the high-level Japan-U.S. talks held on January 2, the Americans made a special request for Japanese cooperation on this issue. Due to various limitations involving distances, flight time, and flight restrictions, it may not be possible to conduct the necessary training at the Atsugi, Misawa, and Iwakuni air bases, where simulated carrier-landing practice is currently being done. Hence it may be necessary to acquire carrier-landing practice facilities in the Kanto area or surrounding region.

In February 1980, Japan's Maritime Self-Defense Force (JMSDF) began participating with other allied naval vessels in RIMPAC (Rim of the Pacific Exercises). These are integrated military exercises planned by the U.S. Third Fleet and conducted approximately every two years. (The February 1980 exercises marked the seventh RIMPAC since they were begun in 1971.) Japanese sea, air, and land units participate in these and other military maneuvers. I have been told by the various U.S. service chiefs that the United States is satisfied with the results of these Japanese military activities.

The downing of a Korean Air passenger aircraft by a Soviet fighter over Sakhalin on September 1, 1983, is an incident that still haunts our memories. On this occasion, the Japanese government provided relevant information to the United States — even though this involved sacrificing certain of its own security interests — and thereby enabled the United States to produce concrete evidence in supporting its condemnation of the Soviet action before the U.N. Security Council. This was commended as another example of Japanese cooperation with the United States. A resolution was even adopted in Congress to express America's gratitude to Japan. This incident was very significant in solidifying the feeling of trust that America has toward Japan.

While on the subject of defense cooperation, special mention must also be made of the agreement that was reached concerning the mutual exchange of military technology (see appendix 1).

Since the advent of the Reagan administration, a viewpoint often articulated by Under Secretary of Defense Delaure (responsible for technological issues) on military technology transfer has become very strong. According to this viewpoint, it is not right for this technology transfer to flow only toward Japan, but rather the flow should be in both directions. Since 1981, American officials have publicly acknowledged their hope of promoting such bidirectional transfer.

Japan has adopted what it calls the *three principles of arms export,* according to which it prohibits exports of military weapons to communist countries, to countries under UN ban, and to countries either involved or likely to be involved in international conflicts. Arms exports to other nations are done reservedly, and military technology is handled in the same manner as the weapons themselves.

The Japanese government was faced with the problem of how to reconcile its three principles with the American contention that it was "unreasonable that Japan, having signed the Japan-U.S. security treaty, should refuse to provide the United States with military technology in the same way it provides that technology to other countries with which it has no such relationship." In

103

January 1983, after studying the issue carefully, Japan decided to open up the way to provide military technology to the United States, making this an exception to its three principles. This position was adopted after acknowledging that the promotion of mutual technological exchange in the defense field between the two nations was extremely crucial in effectively maintaining the Japan-U.S. security structure. On November 8, 1983 (the day before President Reagan arrived in Japan), Japan and the United States concluded an agreement that established basic guidelines for the transfer of Japanese military technology.

From the perspective of Japan-U.S. cooperation, this agreement is to be applauded. At the time, an increasing number of American officials were starting to demand that the United States refuse to provide technology to Japan if Japan would not cooperate in providing technology to the United States.

Toward the end of 1982, Congress voted to place collateral conditions on legislation that forbade the granting of production licenses to foreign countries for weapons made by an arms manufacturer in the state of New York. It seemed that this would have a great impact on Japanese plans to produce the barrel and mount for the M110 self-propelled gun which was to be imported from the United States. This impact was minimized after an all-out effort, but if an agreement had not been reached with respect to providing military technology to the United States, there was good reason to fear that the granting of production licenses to Japan would eventually have been stopped.

Many in Congress and in U.S. industry had second thoughts about this when they concluded that unlimited licensed production and technology transfer were making foreign industry more competitive, thereby narrowing the markets and hurting American industry.

Another argument was that some of the newly emerging industrial nations were making inroads into traditional U.S. arms markets, using technology gained through producing weapons under license agreements. Associated with this was a concern to prevent indiscriminate proliferation, fearing that making technology transfer too easy and increasing the number of arms-exporting countries would in and of itself increase the risk of international conflict.

The U.S. Defense Department has recently been disturbed over

104

the problem of legal and illegal technology transfers to communist countries. This has led to the tightening of COCOM sanctions, and is the reason why, in revising export-control legislation, it was decided (after a long power struggle within the government) that Defense would also have a say in the granting of export licenses. This had previously been the exclusive province of the Commerce Department. Allusion was frequently made to a case in which helicopters manufactured by Hughes in the United States were exported to Europe only to be resold to North Korea. This kind of thing further promoted the tightening of sanctions. For these and other reasons, it could happen that Americans will become more circumspect, not to say nervous, about technology transfers.

I have already argued that the Reagan administration has been more pragmatic than earlier U.S. administrations in formulating Japan policy, and the SS20 problem is another case in point.

In carrying on the INF negotiations with the Soviet Union, the United States position initially seemed to be that the Soviet SS20s simply constituted a problem for the European front. Japan was worried, however, that SS20s removed from Europe could be redeployed in Asia. With the SS20s currently deployed in Siberia, Japan contended that this was not a problem for the European front, but rather a problem that must be addressed from a global perspective, particularly in view of the mobility of the SS20 missile. The Japanese continually reiterated this contention to U.S. officials.

The Americans gave full recognition to the Japanese position, declaring that the United States would pursue the INF negotiations from a global perspective with due consideration given to Asia. This stance has been firmly maintained throughout subsequent arms talks.

Why have U.S. officials been so inclined to weigh Japanese positions concerning defense issues, and to formulate policy with such careful regard to those positions? I venture to say that it is because Japan's steady efforts in the defense field and its cooperation in sharing military technology have engendered a greater American appreciation of Japan's reliability as an ally.

According to an opinion poll conducted at the end of February 1985, by Potomac Associates and the Gallup Organization, the foreign country about which most Americans had a good opinion was Canada (78%, up from 75% in a 1980 survey), followed by Australia (49%, unchanged), Japan (35%, up from 30%), West Germany (34%, up from 33%), Israel (29%, up from 28%), and New Zealand (27%, down from 28%). Japan thus gained 5% over 5 years in this popularity poll to move into third place. Statistically speaking, 5 percentage points represents quite a significant change. This popularity growth seems even more impressive in view of the "Japan bashing" hysteria being stirred up in Congress about the time the 1985 survey was made. (The Japan-censuring measure proposed by Senator Danforth was adopted in late March, but anti-Japan sentiment had been gradually building up in congressional hearings and elsewhere since about January.)

On the question of which countries should be considered extremely important in terms of America's own national interest, Canada was first (77% in 1985, 76% in 1979), the Soviet Union second (68%, 67%), and Japan third (62%, 58%), followed by West Germany (58%) and China (55%).

The seriousness with which Americans view Japan also appeared in response to a question asking which countries, if attacked, would the United States aid by force of arms, 76% of the respondents named the main European allies (up from 69% in a 1984 survey), 70% named Japan (up from 59%), 70% named Australia (up from 64%), and 63% named the Philippines (up from 58%). The figures in support of aiding the main European allies and Japan were the highest ever recorded.

The United States struggled to overcome the aftereffects of the Vietnam War throughout the 1970s. The Reagan administration was said to herald the "rehabilitation" of the Vietnam War, and America was thought to have finally rid itself of the aftereffects of that war. Even during the Reagan years, however, Americans have proven to be almost pathologically gun-shy toward deploying U.S. military forces overseas. That — in spite of this fact — Americans should express strong support for using military power in support of American allies would seem to point to a recovery of self-confidence and a recognition of the importance of standing behind the allies.

The Potomac-Gallup poll also surveyed opinions concerning the U.S. military forces stationed in Europe and Japan. Some 9% of the respondents favored strengthening U.S. forces in Europe (unchanged from 9% in a 1978 survey), 64% favored maintaining current levels (up from 59%), and 16% favored reducing those forces (up from 14%). Some 6% favored strengthening the U.S. forces in Japan (unchanged), 64% favored maintaining current levels (up from 58%), and 18% favored reductions (up from 15%). Thus the numbers of those favoring either maintaining or enhancing current force levels in Japan and in Europe, respectively, are no longer all that disparate. When it comes to the question of defense, therefore, the importance in American minds of Japan has come to rival that of Western Europe.

The poll also contained a question concerning Japanese defense efforts.

> The self-defense forces which Japan can maintain are limited by provisions in its constitution. Some people think that Japan should depend less on the United States and do more to strengthen its own defense forces. Others believe that Japanese rearmament would, on the contrary, pose a threat to the allied nations. Do you think Japan should strengthen its defense forces or not strengthen them?

Of those responding, 52% (down from 56% in 1982) said Japan should strengthen its forces, 40% (up from 26%) said Japan should not do so.

According to the interpretation of William Watts, president of Potomac Associates, more than half of those polled are in favor of Japan strengthening its own defense forces. This group represents various points of view, from those who argue that limiting defense spending to 1% of GNP is ridiculous, to those who urge Japan to play a more active and responsible role in defending itself. Nevertheless, one detects a slight change in the past few years in American attitudes toward Japanese stronger defense capability.

The spread between the defense increase-support group and the opposition group, for instance, narrowed from 30 points to 21 points in just three years. According to one explanation of this trend, just as American workers have been threatened by the influx of Japanese goods into the U.S. marketplace, so now more Americans are fearful lest Japan develop into a strong military presence as well as a powerful economic one. When the economic crisis mentality increases so do the old memories of militaristic imperial Japan.

Since the Reagan administration took office, the Department of Defense has avoided exerting overt pressure on Japan, pursuing rather a course of quiet persuasion in urging the Japanese to steadily build up their defense forces. The Department of Defense attitude has assumed that Japan would take the initiative in carrying out its proper roles and missions in the world. This attitude represents a political savoir-faire that is based on a sound understanding of political realities in Japan. At the same time, however, there are evidently some in America who entertain complex feelings about Japan strengthening its defenses.

The strategic defense initiative (SDI) which has been personally promoted by President Reagan, was initially received rather negatively, both in the United States and internationally. The plan has been pushed steadily along behind the president's strong support, however, and attention has come to be focused on America's allies.

Since visiting the United States and meeting with President Reagan at Camp David in December 1984, Prime Minister Margaret Thatcher of the United Kingdom has expressed support for SDI research and development, stating that the United States should consult with the Soviet Union concerning actual deployment and drawing no little international attention with her position.

It was against this background that the subject of SDI was broached at the Japan-U.S. summit talks held in January 1985.

Secretary of State Shultz took quite a bit of time in explaining SDI at the breakfast talks that were held between him and Foreign Minister Abe. President Reagan felt a moral obligation to push forward with SDI, explained Shultz, in the interest of bringing the nuclear arms race to a halt.

At the summit talks with Prime Minister Nakasone, President Reagan explained very carefully that SDI is not nuclear weaponry, but defensive weaponry. After listening to this explanation, Nakasone indicated that he understood the need for SDI research.

After Nakasone and Abe returned to Japan, SDI was discussed and debated from every possible angle, in the Diet and elsewhere. The prime minister and the Japanese government have consistently insisted that they have gone no farther than expressing understanding of the SDI concept and SDI research.

Observers next turned their attention to the Bonn Summit, held in May, to see how SDI would be dealt with there. All that came out of these meetings, however, on the subject of SDI, were the following remarks of Chairman Kohl in his summarizing statement.

> We discussed the East-West problem and the issue of SDI, which is advocated by the U.S. president. The President described his long-range research plans. He also expressed a willingness to conduct close consultations now and into the future, however, which to me is most welcome, and the point I should like to emphasize. The American president stressed that he is not seeking a dominant position for the United States, but rather the establishment of strategic stability.

The cautious attitudes being taken toward SDI by the European allies, and by the United Kingdom and France in particular, are thought to be informed by misgivings as to what the fundamental strategic impact of actual SDI development would be on them as nuclear powers (in the cases of the UK and France). The question now is how mutual understanding can be deepened and solidarity strengthened among the European powers that currently entertain such apprehensions.

The United States, more recently, has been appealing to all nations to participate in SDI research. This is likely to require very deliberate and careful study, from many different perspectives, including the question of the significance of such research for technological development.

One hears, finally, the argument from some that Japan need not build up its defense forces if it will only increase its budget for economic cooperation. From others one hears the argument that economic friction might disappear if Japan were to increase its defense budget. I find both of these arguments hard to swallow.

From the standpoint of overall national security, it is absolutely imperative that we strengthen economic cooperation, but this by itself will not suffice to defend Japan. Nor is economic friction the kind of thing that will go away just because we have increased spending on defense or on economic cooperation.

There is no question but that Japan must respond to international expectations in playing a more active international role. In doing so, however, she must not lose sight of the fundamental nature of the economic frictions which are now so troublesome. I grant that, in certain respects, the defense problem, the economic cooperation problem, and the trade problem are all interrelated. Fundamentally, however, they are distinctly different problems, having different origins and different implications. Hence each of them must eventually be resolved within its own particular sphere. Only then can policy be founded on more universal considerations.

Appendix 3

In 1981, at the urging of American officials, Japan also began to study the problem of transferring military technology to the United States. The basic problem was how to reconcile Japan's "three principles of arms export" with the Japan-U.S. security arrangement. After about a year and a half of cautious negotiating, it was concluded, on January 14, 1983, that the way would be opened to provide military technology to the United States, handling this as an exception to the three principles. This decision of the government was announced by the Chief Cabinet Secretary. Then, on November 8, 1983, a Communiqué Based on the Mutual Defense Assistance Agreement was signed. This document set forth basic guidelines for actually transferring military technology to the United States. In determining the specific details of such transfers, very careful procedures must be taken through a Joint Military Technology Commission (JMTC) which the Communiqué provides for. The first JMTC meeting was held on November 6, 1984. Relevant governmental position statements and official documents are summarized below.

Three Principles of Arms Export

The approval of the Minister of International Trade and Industry is required by the Foreign Exchange Act, the Foreign Trade Control Act (1949 Law No. 228), and the Export Trade Control Order (1949 Government Order No. 378) for the exportation of "weapons."

The three principles of arms export were set forth by Prime Minister Eisaku Sato before the Lower House Audit Committee on April 21, 1967. These principles clearly state that the government, in enforcing the Foreign Exchange Act, etc., shall not permit arms exports to (1) communist bloc nations, (2) nations (such as the Republic of South Africa) banned by the United Nations as recipients of arms exports, and (3) nations involved or in danger of becoming involved in international conflicts.

Unified Policy on Weapons Exports

On February 27, 1976, Prime Minister Takeo Miki set forth the following points before the Lower House Audit Committee.

1. *Government Policy.* Japan, as a peaceful nation, has handled the exportation of "weapons" very circumspectly, and it will continue to handle such exportation according to the following policy positions, and will not promote such exportation. (1) The exportation of "weapons" to regions covered by the *three principles* will not be allowed. (2) Even to regions not covered by the *three principles,* the exportation of "weapons" shall be discouraged, in keeping with the spirit of the Constitution, the Foreign Exchange Act, and the Trade Control Act. (3) The exportation of equipment for manufacturing weapons (according to the provisions of the Export Trade Control Order, Attached Table 1, Paragraph 109) shall be treated in the same manner as the exportation of "weapons."

2. *Weapons Defined.* (1) By "weapons," in the three principles of arms export, are meant "things that are used by military personnel and which make a direct contribution to battle." Specifically, those things which, among the things listed from Paragraphs 197 to 205 in Table 1 of the Export Trade Control Order, satisfy this definition are "weapons." (2) As found in the language of the Self-Defense Act, the term "weapons" is understood to refer to "firearms, gunpowder, swords, and other machines, implements, and devices that are for the purpose of either directly inflicting harm to persons or destroying objects when used as means of carrying on military battles." Naval escort vessels, fighter aircraft, and tanks are believed to satisfy the above definition of "weapons."

LEGISLATIVE DECISIONS PERTAINING
TO WEAPONS EXPORTS (Lower House Plenary Session 3/20/81; Upper House Plenary Session 3/31/81)

Japan, in keeping with its position as a peaceful nation, and with its peaceful ideals as reflected in the Japanese Constitution, has handled the matter of arms exports very cautiously, according to the three principles of arms exports and the unified governmental policy outlined in 1976. That, notwithstanding, situations have recently developed that are in violation of these policies and principles is most deplorable. Be it therefore resolved that the government shall take a strict and cautious attitude in handling the matter of arms exports and shall implement effective measures, including organizational reforms, to that end.

REMARKS OF CHIEF CABINET SECRETARY ON PROVIDING MILITARY TECHNOLOGY TO UNITED STATES (1/14/83)

Since June 1981, the U.S. government has been requesting reciprocal technological exchange between Japan and the United States in the defense field. After long and careful deliberation within the government over the specific issue of providing military technology to the United States, we have now arrived at the following conclusions, which were approved today in a meeting of the Cabinet.

1. Under the Japan-U.S. security arrangement, Japan and the United States are to cooperate with each other in maintaining and developing their respective defense forces. Thus far, in the way of improving defense capability, Japan has received various kinds of cooperation from the United States, including the provision of technology. In consideration of the current situation, and especially the rise in recent years of Japan's technological level, it is now evident that it has become extremely important, in the interest of effectively managing the Japan-U.S. security arrangement, for Japan to promote reciprocal technological exchange with the United States in the field of defense. To do so is in keeping with the spirit of the Japan-U.S. Security Treaty and related agreements that prescribe reciprocal cooperation between the two nations in the defense field. To do so will also contribute to the peace and security of Japan and the Far East.

2. The government has thus far handled the matter of military exports according to the three principles of arms export (which includes the governmental policy statement on arms exports of February 27, 1976). In view of the foregoing considerations, however, and in response to U.S. requests, we have decided to open the way to transfer military technology (including items falling

113

under the category of weapons when they are necessary to make such transfer effective) to the United States as a part of the aforesaid reciprocal exchange. In making such transfers, the three principles of arms export shall not apply. In such cases, such transfers shall be implemented within certain guidelines that are based on relevant provisions of the Japan-U.S. Mutual Defense Assistance Agreement. By so doing, the basic ideal of a peaceful nation, namely the avoidance of lending assistance to nations engaged in international conflict, as set forth in the three principles of arms export, shall be firmly maintained.

3. It goes without saying, moreover, that it is the government's intention to continue to firmly uphold the three principles of arms export, and to respect the spirit of the resolution on the arms export problem which the Diet passed in March 1981.

SUMMARY OF COMMUNIQUÉ ON PROVIDING MILITARY TECHNOLOGY TO UNITED STATES (11/8/83)

1. The Government of Japan, in accord with the detailed provisions jointly adopted for the purpose of implementing this agreement, and in accord with relevant laws and government orders, approves the transfer to the United States government of such military technology as is necessary to enhance the defense capabilities of the United States, and which is set forth below under (2).

2. A Joint Military Technology Commission (JMTC) is to be established as a consultative body between the governments of Japan and the United States with respect to the implementation of this agreement, and is to be made up of separate national committees from Japan and the United States. The Japanese committee, based on information received from the U.S. committee and on deliberations in the JMTC, shall determine what military technology is suitable for recognition by the Government of Japan for transfer to the United States.

3. Detailed provisions for the purpose of implementing this agreement shall be jointly adopted by duly authorized representatives of the two governments.

4. With respect to aid that is provided, this agreement shall be implemented in accord with the Mutual Defense Assistance Agreement, which (i) prohibits any use thereof that is inconsistent with the United Nations Charter, (ii) prohibits any use thereof for other purposes, and (iii) prohibits the transfer thereof to any third nation without prior consent.

5. The U.S. government agrees to implement secrecy safeguarding measures that will guarantee that secrets are afforded the same secrecy classifications as are afforded under the secrecy safeguards provided for in Japan, and that these measures will be enforced in the United States with respect to the military technology that is provided.

10

Becoming an
"International" Nation

To briefly summarize what has been said so far, the strong dissatisfaction that some Americans feel toward Japan is informed by the sense of impending danger and crisis — in the face of Japanese competition — which is so deeply rooted in U.S. industry and labor.

In Congress there are feelings of suspicion and distrust that have developed in the course of U.S. trade negotiations with Japan over the past several years.

While we Japanese have our own opinions on these matters, so long as these ideas and feelings are embraced in America, and particularly in Congress, Japan must recognize them realistically for what they are, and act accordingly. The critical question is how, specifically, these suspicions of Japanese intentions and these fears of Japanese competition are to be allayed.

On these points, the recent testimony of Lionel Olmer before Congress and congressional action in response thereto are instructive.

Under Secretary of Commerce Olmer, after conducting intense negotiations with the Japanese over the telecommunications issue as part of the four-sector MOSS negotiations, testified before Congress. After carefully explaining the specific U.S. demands and the concrete progress that was made, Olmer testified concerning the active measures that Japan was taking in response.

As a result of the Olmer testimony — according to U.S. officials close to this situation — even some of the most resolute congressional Japan bashers began to soften their tone against Japan and to exhibit a greater measure of understanding toward the Japanese position.

As such incidents clearly demonstrate, Japan must make maximal cooperative efforts to insure that American negotiators will be satisfied and be able to confidently report their negotiating successes to Congress. And, even if everything cannot be completely resolved at once, it is absolutely essential that concrete measures be taken, step by step, to eliminate the more glaring symbols of Japanese market exclusionism and to deal with other problems that the United States has with Japan.

After studying the matter carefully from every possible angle, Nissan Motor Co. boldly decided on the acquisition of a Cray XMP-11 supercomputer. Quite aside from the question of cost, this action was very significant because of the favorable impression that it made on American officials.

The "tall container" problem continued to be a thorn in the flesh of the Americans for a long time. The issue was taken up by the OTO, but no satisfactory results were forthcoming. Finally, however, the tireless labors and cooperation of the officials involved paid off, and a way of resolving the problem was found. This was one more step toward improved Japan-U.S. relations.

But what about the sense of crisis and intimidation that those in American industry and labor harbor in the face of Japanese competition? When we examine this issue in view of the difference in the speed of economic recovery in Japan and the United States, and of the exchange rate factor, we are forced to conclude that, so long as America's phenomenally great domestic demand continues and no protectionist sanctions are implemented, superior Japanese goods — supported by high productivity and strong competitiveness — will continue to flow into U.S. markets, and that flow will be unstoppable. To the extent that these conditions prevail, we can only expect the trade imbalance to continue, and cannot realistically hope to end the ongoing friction between the two most economically powerful nations in the world.

Hence it will be no easy task to dispel American fears of Japanese competition. For Japan's part, however, behavior that is condemned as "unfair" and "breaking the rules of the game" must be corrected with all possible haste. In the area of trade, concentrated high-volume export practices that adversely impact related American industries and grant them no quarter must be avoided. Japan must by all means maintain a consistent policy of *reasonable* exports.

It is also desirable, of course, that the United States take aggressive measures to rectify its enormous fiscal deficit, and thereby bring interest rates back down to normal and correct the current strong-dollar situation.

On April 9, 1985 the Japanese government announced its 7th economic policy measures, in conjunction with which an "action plan" is to be drafted in July. Those who appreciate the importance of the issues we have been discussing will be watching anxiously to see what kind of concrete measures are worked into the action plan, because that will have a decisive impact on future Japan-U.S. economic relations. If the finished action plan gives the impression in America, and particularly in Congress, of being just another compendium of half-hearted stop-gap measures, then we must brace ourselves against the retaliatory measures that the United States will inevitably take in order to demonstrate that she is no paper tiger.

We are glad to see, at least on the surface, some softening of the anti-Japanese rhetoric in Congress which, for a while, had emotions running very high. We have recently begun to see more members of Congress who understand the importance of Japan-U.S. relations, and who take a more objective and cool-headed approach to our mutual problems. The mood that was making members of Congress reluctant to speak out against denunciations of Japan has been dispelled to some extent, and it is now possible to carry on more constructive debates. It is very important that this trend not be reversed.

One of America's complaints is that, in the area of research and development, Japan totally neglects basic research and pours all of its energy into applications R & D that leads directly to commercialization. I have often had to listen to the argument that Japan ought to do its own basic research, that applications R & D properly must grow out of basic research.

Many Americans now believe that U.S. industry has done itself great harm by the granting of production licenses and the transferring of technology, which have gone on almost indiscriminately thus far, giving Japanese and other foreign industries tremendous competitiveness. To put it another way, I think that there is now a widespread sense among Americans that the basic competitive position that the United States has vis-à-vis Japan must not be allowed to become detrimental to U.S. industry itself.

Considering things in the light of this fundamental American complaint, Japanese industry should not limit its efforts to applications R & D, but rather place more emphasis than it traditionally has on basic research. Technology transfers should flow in both directions, not just toward Japan. And unless greater effort is made to make this happen, we must not be surprised if American research institutions—including the laboratories of famous schools of technology—close their doors to Japanese researchers, ostensibly in the interest of national security. The trend toward refusing to provide research data to Japan could also be accelerated, which would seriously hamper Japanese R & D efforts in advanced technological fields.

By taking adequate institutionalizing measures in these areas of concern, and eliminating the objects of criticism one by one, Japan can put itself in a position to challenge American censure with greater confidence. By taking such a high-ground position, Japan could then do more than merely urge U.S. authorities to adopt certain macro-economic policies. Japanese officials would then carry more weight when they contended that American businesses were not working hard enough to develop Japanese markets, and when they urged those businesses to be more aggressive.

It may be argued that U.S. industry has historically developed and been supported by an enormous domestic market, as a consequence of which American business circles lack sufficient knowledge and experience concerning exporting their products abroad. I think that this is a fair assessment, which is particularly valid for small or medium-sized businesses. The latter recently seem to have become much more aware of the importance of overseas markets. That is encouraging, and one hopes that more U.S. businesses will work much harder to develop overseas markets. The seller's market mentality, however, which overestimates the inherent appeal of "superior" American-made products, continues to be strong in the United States. That approach is doomed to failure in Japan's highly selective buyer's market. Japanese officials keep arguing that American businessmen must change this self-defeating attitude. If Japan takes visible steps to open its markets, however, these arguments will be much more persuasive and effective.

Turning to areas other than direct trade, I must again mention the great importance of direct investment in the United States. Every time I meet with American state governors I am deeply impressed with the zeal of American officials in enticing Japanese companies to invest directly in America.

Having campaigned for the liberalization of Japan's financial markets and the internationalization of the yen, U.S. officials applaud the progress that has been made through the Yen-Dollar Committee's report-drafting work. America's own financial institutions are not altogether satisfied, however, partly because of problems concerning the reconfiguration of Japan's financial markets. I think Japan should go even further with its liberalizing measures. This is not a matter that can be resolved with some kind of one-shot, quick-fix, all-powerful remedy. As painful as the process may be, Japan must correct its image as an unfair player by eliminating one by one the "little" things that are so nettlesome to Americans and that aggravate their suspicions.

As became apparent during the debates in the congressional hearings, America's fundamental dissatisfaction with Japan is framed by a perception of Japan as a nation that fails to appreciate that it has become an enormously powerful economic entity that has international obligations it must fulfill. This perception underlies the charge that Japan is also failing to contribute as it ought in maintaining the international trading order.

Here again, I believe that we Japanese must seriously and honestly consider the American position, resolve to fulfill our international obligations, and then take whatever aggressive action is necessary to do so.

The problem cannot be dismissed by claiming that the situation is hopeless because "Americans just don't make anything that Japanese consumers want to buy." To persist in holding that view will only leave Japan isolated from the rest of the international community. In addressing the problem, there must be constant attention to what effect Japanese actions will have internationally and what responsibilities Japan must fulfill in promoting world peace and prosperity.

The non-economic field in which America expects Japan to do much more is, of course, defense. There has long been a strong undercurrent of feeling in the United States that the allied nations ought to have to bear the defense burden equally with the United States, according to their respective capacities. Senator Sam

Nunn (Democrat, Georgia), a powerful member of the Senate Armed Services Committee, has proposed legislation that would mandate reductions in American troop levels in Europe if adequate cooperation is not forthcoming from the European allies. The same sort of viewpoint was reflected when President Jimmy Carter proposed, shortly after his inauguration, the complete withdrawal of U.S. forces from the Republic of Korea (although the Carter administration subsequently altered course and decided to maintain the current status).

Since the 1970s, Japan has worked steadily to intensify its defense efforts. From America's perspective, however, Japan has an international responsibility — as a member of the western alliance, and particularly as the second most powerful economy in the world — to do much more to build up its defense capabilities. This American perspective has been sharpened by such unsettling international developments as the Soviet invasion of Afghanistan and the Vietnamese armed incursion into Cambodia which was backed by the Soviet Union. In view of the fact that the Japanese have such a strong vested interest in the security of their trading routes, it is also widely held that Japan — even if purely in its own economic self-interest — should take a more active role in defending its sea lanes out to a distance of 1,000 nautical miles, as the government in Tokyo has promised to do.

This view leads to the argument that the Japanese government should naturally expedite its implementation of the Defense Planning Guidelines. The Reagan administration has studiously avoided pressuring the Japanese government to bolster its defense effort in specific numerical terms (as was done during the Carter administration), but there is no question that it expects Japan to do more in upgrading its defense capabilities, holding that Japan has an international obligation to do so.

In his national defense report to Congress for fiscal 1986, submitted in February, Secretary of Defense Weinberger emphasized that Japan was spending more than $1.1 billion annually to defray the cost of maintaining U.S. military forces on its soil, and spoke in commendation of Japanese defense efforts. However, in the 1985 report on the status of defense efforts among the allied nations, which was made public in early May, Japan was specifically cited for the poor battle-sustaining capabilities of its self-defense forces. From this alone it is evident that Japan is thought abroad to have made inadequate provisions against possible external threats. The conviction that each of the allies should shoulder its own responsibilities runs very deeply in Congress. Continuing demands for fair play in the economic arena will no doubt be accompanied by demands that Japan do its "fair share" in making more strenuous defense efforts.

Paralleling these demands in the defense field are expectations that Japan will do more in the area of economic foreign aid.

Congress has so far taken a relatively passive attitude toward foreign aid as administered through international agencies, and the administration in Washington has been in no position to campaign for increased economic aid against congressional opposition, particularly in view of the enormous domestic problem posed by America's fiscal deficit. Japan, on the other hand, widely thought to be basking in relative economic opulence, is now expected to beef up its economic aid programs.

American officials are very happy to see Japan moving now beyond the Asian region — which it has traditionally focused on — and actively extending economic assistance to such countries as Pakistan, Turkey, Egypt, and even Jamaica. Expectations are high that Japan will broaden the scope of this economic cooperation even farther.

Since economic friction began to heat up, Japan has been urged to strengthen its economic aid programs in general, and ODA (official development assistance) in particular.

It is also now being stressed in the United States that Japan should become more actively involved in solving the problem of debt accumulation that the developing nations are facing, and that Japan should take resolute measures to increase its imports of finished goods from developing nations. This emphasis came out in Senator Danforth's comments to me on the occasion of my parting visit to him. "The United States is working hard to resolve the problem of accumulated debt in the developing nations," said Danforth. "Accordingly, even though we are confronted with tremendous domestic barriers, we are endeavoring to increase our imports from those developing nations, and currently receive 58 percent of the manufactured goods which they export throughout the world. By comparison, Japan receives no more than 8 percent of these exports from the developing nations. Shouldn't Japan take its international obligations a little more seriously?"

In considering the north-south problem, we should remember the frequently repeated position of the southern nations, namely, that aid is appreciated but what is really needed is trade.

Of great importance also is that Japan play a much more active role in the international political arena than it has in the past. During the 1983 Williamsburg summit, Japan participated actively in drafting the political statement in support of western solidarity. This was commended by the Americans, who said that now Japan was "acting like a true ally." It is through such behind-the-scenes international activity as this that American appreciation for its Japanese ally is enhanced. In the same context, Japan's cooperation with the United States following the shooting down of the Korean Air 747 in September 1983, was extremely significant in deepening the sense of trust that Americans now feel toward Japan.

Americans have also given high marks to Japan for taking positions that emphasize its solidarity with the Western allies in implementing economic measures against the Soviet Union, and for using its close diplomatic ties with Tehran and Baghdad—working through official and unofficial channels—to get both sides in the Iran-Iraq war to agree to a partial cease-fire.

Nearly every year since 1960, the Ministry of Foreign Affairs (MOFA) has commissioned the Gallup Organization to conduct a public opinion poll among ordinary Americans to find out how they feel about Japan. According to these annual surveys, the percentage of Americans who trust Japan began to decline in 1980, reaching a ten-year low of 44 percent in 1983. In 1984 this measure of trust rebounded to 57 percent and was only off one point at 56 percent in 1985. (The 1983 nadir is believed to reflect the intense negative coverage that the U.S. media gave Japan-U.S. economic friction that year.)

In a Gallup poll taken in January 1985, more than half of those responding indicated that Japan was a nation that could be trusted. This tallies well with the impressions I got when making a round of visits through the 50 states. I think that this trend reflects an awareness and an approval by Americans of Japan's recent activities in the field of international politics.

Not all of the news is good, however. Together with the general survey, another survey of opinion on Japan has been taken annually since 1972 among intellectuals. This additional survey includes the question "Is the economic relationship with Japan advantageous or threatening to the United States?" Of those responding, 66 percent (67 percent in the previous survey) said "advantageous," but 23 percent (21 percent previously) said "threatening." Thus, in the space of a year, the "advantageous" opinion declined 1 percent while the "threatening" opinion rose 2 percent.

Since intellectuals tend to react more sensitively than people in general, small fluctuations in the survey results could possibly indicate that conditions are ripe for economic friction heating up again, after a short respite.

As to how we should interpret the 66 percent who responded "advantageous," I think it safe to surmise that these respondents represent the American consumer.

U.S. consumer demand has risen rapidly as the economy has recovered, and Japanese products — highly competitive in terms of both price and quality — are responding to this brisk demand. The point has now been reached where Americans are no longer able to enjoy the affluent consumption-oriented lifestyle without Japanese products. From the consumer's perspective, therefore, America's economic relationship with Japan is a plus. It is this, I think, which explains the 66 percent result.

In the previous chapter I alluded in some detail to the results of an opinion poll made by Potomac Associates. On the question of which countries are extremely important to the United States, 77 percent said Canada, 68 percent said the Soviet Union, and 62 percent said Japan. When asked which countries friendly to the United States, if attacked militarily, should U.S. forces be dispatched to defend, 76 percent indicated support for the major European allies, while 70 percent support was registered for Japan and Australia, respectively. These are significant results, particularly when one remembers how long Americans suffered from the aftereffects of the Vietnam War, and the deep reluctance they have shown toward deploying U.S. combat troops overseas. Unable to extricate themselves from the aftereffects of Vietnam (and Watergate) during the Carter administration, Americans had to wait until the Reagan administration had come to power, and the Vietnam War had been rehabilitated, before they could finally do so.

When the bottom-line issue of employment is brought into the picture, however, perceptions are changed. To the question "Which countries' exports of manufactured goods pose a threat to U.S.

employment?" 80 percent of the Americans surveyed answered Japan. This was followed by Taiwan (52 percent) and China (22 percent).

This American fear of Japanese competition is not a new problem. But following the outcries from members of Congress and the censure heaped upon Japan in congressional hearings in January and February, and after these sentiments have been hammered day after day into the minds of Americans through nationwide media coverage, the conviction that Japan poses a real economic threat may be on the rise.

The significance of the survey results cited above cannot be overemphasized. We Japanese must continually bear in mind that the United States is public-opinion oriented, and that U.S. public opinion is fickle. If one backtracks to the sources of Japan-U.S. economic friction, one inevitably runs up against this idea that Japan poses a threat. But part of the problem is that Japanese industry seems to be unaware that it is posing a threat.

When all this has been duly considered, the problem boils down to the fact that the United States and much of the free world expect and demand that Japan undertake its proper responsibilities as a member of the international community. As the second-ranked economic power in the world, Japan will no longer be permitted the luxury of behaving as a small insular kingdom. Every Japanese citizen must become more conscious of Japan's international position, so that Japan can perform its proper international roles.

What then makes a country truly "international," and what specifically does "internationalization" entail?

Statements and actions made in Japan now have a worldwide impact, both politically and economically. In the past, remote and insular Japan was able to go its merry way without giving much thought to what others might think. In today's shrunken world, however, going one's merry way often runs afoul of the rightful interests of one's neighbors. Neither internationally responsible nor mollycoddling behavior is any longer tolerated. Japan, therefore, is no longer able to behave in ways that adversely affect its neighbors and partners. On the positive side, Japan is now expected to act as a positive contributor to the international community. I think that *internationalization* is the process by which every Japanese citizen is made to fully appreciate these realities. When that happens Japan will indeed be an *international* nation.

11

Looking Toward Asia

Since Ronald Reagan became President, there has been a gradual shift in the United States toward placing greater emphasis on Asia and the Pacific basin. This shift may be partially attributed to a number of circumstances, including the fact that Reagan himself is from California's Pacific coast, the fact that he was governor of California for two terms, that fact that he visited Japan as a special envoy of President Richard Nixon, and the fact that George Shultz—appointed Secretary of State in 1982—has strong connections with California and an uncommon interest in Asia and the Pacific. Even at that, however, the new emphasis is quite remarkable when contrasted with what went before.

The Reagan administration cannot claim, of course, to be the original pioneer of this new emphasis. Former Congressman Lester Wolff (Democrat, New York, defeated in the 1982 elections) had already acquitted himself well as a leader of those in Congress calling for greater cooperation with the Asian and Pacific nations. But the trend toward this view does seem to have quickly gathered steam once the Reagan administration came in.

In public addresses given in January and March 1984, Under Secretary of State Lawrence Eagleberger made a number of significant statements. "The center of gravity in American foreign policy is now shifting from American and European affairs toward the Pacific region, and particularly toward affairs with Japan," declared Eagleberger. "Since 1978, U.S. trade with the Pacific region has surpassed U.S. trade with Europe. In 1982 the margin amounted to $13 billion. The combined GNP of US and Japan now accounts for almost a third of world GNP, and Japan is second only to Canada as a purchaser of American goods."

Eagleberger thus stressed that America's future lay increasingly in Asia and the Pacific, both politically and economically. Not surprisingly, these addresses in early 1984 grated on European nerves (See appendix 4).

Eagleberger, though ostensibly a member of the "European school," had already experienced hard times in negotiating with the Europeans on a number of issues, including the implementation of sanctions against the Soviet Union, and the deployment of the Pershing II missiles. Some even surmised that Eagleberger's dissatisfaction with European attitudes on those issues led to his strong support for giving greater priority to Asia and the Pacific.

There were concerns that feelings between the United States and Europe might deteriorate further, so Deputy Secretary of State Kenneth Dam gave a speech in Chicago in August 1984, in which he made the following conciliatory statements. "We are not involved in a zero-sum game of choosing either Europe or the Asian-Pacific region. If that were the case, then our emphasis on the Pacific might result in a lowering of Europe's relative position. But U.S. foreign policy is not a zero-sum game. It is the foreign policy of the United States to increasingly promote and maintain the traditionally deep relations with Europe while squarely confronting the importance of Asia and the Pacific which circumstances now dictate."

Shortly after succeeding Eagleberger as Under Secretary of State in May 1984, Michael Armacost (former U.S. Ambassador to the Philippines) visited the major European allied nations. Armacost had been relatively uninvolved with European affairs previous to this, and these visits were made partly in the interest of better mutual understanding between himself and the major European foreign ministers. I think they were also intended to convey a message from the Reagan administration to the effect that there would be no fundamental change in America's traditional stance of placing emphasis on Europe.

Nevertheless, the idea that the future lies in Asia and the Pacific—as Ambassador Mike Mansfield began asserting quite some time ago—has gradually but unmistakably come to be widely accepted in the United States.

Many Europeans express dissatisfaction with America's European policy, and complain that the main policy-making figures in the Reagan administration lack adequate understanding of and experience in Europe. This probably reflects European resentment over the trends they now see in American public opinion.

Japan quickly decided to participate in the Association of South-East Asian Nations (ASEAN) Extended Foreign Ministers' Conference held in June 1978, and made plain its position on the importance of ASEAN. The United States had not at that time yet consolidated its official position on ASEAN. This may have been partly due to a kind of "let's-stay-out-of-Asia" psychology which was operative in America in the immediate aftermath of the Vietnam War.

The predominant view among the leaders of the ASEAN nations themselves, however, was that, given the fluidity of the political situation in Asia, the American presence was absolutely necessary for stable development. As a result of this majority view, the United States was asked to participate in the Extended Foreign Ministers' Conference. American participation began in the 2nd Extended Foreign Ministers' Conference, held in July 1979. Since then, Secretaries of State Cyrus Vance, Edmund Muskie, Alexander Haig, and George Shultz have each attended.

At a meeting of the Los Angeles World Affairs Council in October 1984, Shultz made a speech entitled "A Forward Look at Foreign Policy" in which he gave a broad overview of how the foreign policy achievements of the first Reagan term would be built on and further developed in the second term. "Today, a sense of Pacific community is emerging with the potential for greater collaboration among many nations with an extraordinary diversity of ocultures, race, and political systems," said Shultz. "Certainly this is not as institutionalized as our ties with Europe, but there is an expanding practice of consultation, a developing sense of common interest, and an exciting vision of the future. We may well be at the threshold of a new era in international relations in the Pacific Basin." This speech drew much attention as a reconfirmation of America's recent foreign policy stance of attaching more importance to Asia.

It is of course apparent that the United States government does not think that this Pacific community idea could be given an organizational framework right away, but it is equally apparent that its basic policy for the Asian-Pacific region is to pioneer and develop the possibilities for such a community through gradually increasing the level of cooperation with the nations of that region. One preliminary step taken in that direction was the appointment of Richard Fairbanks (who had participated in the Middle East peace talks as an advisor to the Secretary of State) as a roving ambassador to the Asian-Pacific region. The significance of Fairbanks' diplomatic visits throughout the region should be noted in seeking to understand the Asian policy of the United States.

One other noteworthy aspect of the Reagan administration's Asian-Pacific policy is the pivotal position delegated to Japan. This acknowledgment was firmly established after conducting a basic reevaluation of U.S. policy on the region. There is a tendency among Americans to think first of China when the subject of Asia is brought up, and they express keen interest in the modernization measures that the Chinese government is now promoting. Nevertheless, the important position occupied by Japan is openly acknowledged—a fact that we must not lose sight of.

Turning to private-sector organizations in this area, there is the Pacific Basin Economic Council (PBEC), through which business leaders address themselves to Asian-Pacific problems, and the Pacific Economic Cooperation Conference (PECC), which is made up of figures from government, the business world, and academia. Both organizations are participated in by Japan, the United States, Canada, Australia, and New Zealand, and have a long history of activity, discussing at the private level ways of enhancing cooperation in the Pacific region. (Government officials do participate in PECC, but not as official representatives of their governments. They attend only in the capacity of private individuals.)

Although there has been some talk of merging PBEC and PECC into a single organization, we should be conscious of the differences in their backgrounds and orientations. At any rate, the Reagan administration's policy is to continue supporting the activities of such nongovernmental organizations in seeking greater cooperation in the Asian-Pacific region.

Governor George Ariyoshi of Hawaii, with the support of Senator Spark Matsunaga of the same state, is promoting a plan to establish the Hawaii Technology Center. The primary objective is to strengthen the ties between Hawaii and the South Pacific island nations through technological aid, as part of future Asia-Pacific cooperation. Not only is Hawaii close to these nations geographically, but strong personal ties have been developed as well because many leaders from the South Pacific have studied at the Hawaii East-West Center. Many new projects are expected to be undertaken in the United States in preparation for the coming Asian-Pacific age.

Appendix 4

Brief synopses are given below of speeches made by prominent U.S. Department of State officials which deal with the importance now given to the Pacific region.

SPEECH BY UNDER SECRETARY OF STATE EAGLEBERGER AT CONFERENCE SPONSORED BY THE JOHN DAVIS LODGE INTERNATIONAL CENTER (1/31/84)

The center of gravity in U.S. foreign policy is now shifting from American and European relations toward the Pacific region, and particularly toward relations with Japan. This in itself is not a bad thing, but we must carefully consider the effects which this shift is bringing about.

Firstly, the volume of trade done with the Pacific region last year surpassed, for the first time, that done with Europe. Secondly, the U.S. population is shifting from the East Coast to the West Coast, resulting in changes in American views on foreign policy.

For the balance of this century, no matter what else might change in the world, the mutual defense ties that stretch across the Pacific Ocean will continue to be absolutely essential to the preservation of peace. At the same time, the center of gravity in U.S. foreign policy is shifting toward the Pacific region. During the next twenty years, the United States and Japan may become the foremost competitors in the field of technological development, but they could also become the foremost collaborators in this field. If in the meantime the Western European nations persist with the old policies of the past, they may find themselves left out of this technological competition and cooperation.

Accordingly, we are faced with the problem of how, over the next twenty years, to coordinate our relations with Western Europe and our relations with the Japan-Pacific region as the latter becomes increasingly powerful economically.

If we fail to handle this problem we may find that while we have been redoubling our efforts to maintain close ties with Western Europe (perhaps with nothing to show for it in the end), our relationship with the Pacific region has become firmly established.

During the course of these developments, those charged with making and implementing government policy will have to face many problems that will be very difficult to handle.

EAGLEBERGER SPEECH TO NATIONAL ASSOCIATION OF NEWSPAPER EDITORS (3/7/84)

It is not my purpose to say that NATO is on the brink of a crisis. The fifteen years remaining in this century will be years of change, however, and I believe that we now have a good opportunity to study and determine how the alliance should deal with the coming changes.

One of the changes that will take place during these years will be the movement of populations within the United States. The center of the population—and with it the political center of gravity—has been shifting steadily toward the West Coast ever since the first national census was taken. If California were a country instead of a state, it would have one of the highest GNP's in the world. The supremacy of the eastern cities (New York, etc.) is now either challenged or eclipsed by the western cities (Los Angeles, San Francisco, etc.).

Pacific economic dynamism is not limited to the United States. Asia has now become the most economically prosperous region in the world. Japanese products are sold all over the globe. The dynamic market economies of the ASEAN nations and of the Republic of Korea, Taiwan, and Hong Kong are now producing quality merchandise which is price-competitive in world markets. And China's economic potential is enormous.

Since 1978, trade with the Pacific region has surpassed trade with Europe—in 1982 by a margin of $13 billion. Japan and U.S. GNP combined now represents one-third of world GNP, and Japan is second only to Canada as a purchaser of American products.

Japan and the United States, moreover, now play the most im-

132

portant roles in the field of high-tech R & D. In the 21st century, these two nations will probably be either competitors or partners.

The United States will be faced with the necessity of creating and maintaining institutional links with its Asian friends — links that meet both U.S. and Asian needs. These links will not be the same, however, as those that exist with America's European friends. The closer ties with Asia cannot duplicate the historical relationship that the United States has with Europe.

SPEECH BY DEPUTY SECRETARY OF STATE KENNETH DAM ENTITLED "EUROPE VERSUS ASIA — IS FOREIGN POLICY A ZERO-SUM GAME?" (Chicago, 8/6/84)

The argument that America's central focus is shifting from Europe toward Asia presents a number of fundamental questions. Firstly, is such a transition actually taking place? Secondly, assuming that it is taking place, is it a cause or is it a result of the growing divergence in politics between the United States and its European allies? And thirdly, confronted with that situation, how can the advanced democracies of Europe, North America, and Asia continue to counter the common threats to their prosperity and peace.

My own view on these issues is that international problems are not a zero-sum game. Undeniably, changes are occurring in Europe and Asia, and also in U.S. relations with those two regions. But United States policy is not biased toward either region; it is balanced. It is true that Asia's importance — politically, in terms of mutual defense, and especially economically — is rising. But it does not follow that strengthened relations with Asia must cause America's traditional ties with Europe to be weakened. On the contrary, in the area of foreign policy, the Reagan administration has been very successful in persuading the advanced democracies of Europe, Asia, and North America to cooperate in promoting global resolutions to their common economic and security problems.

I believe that United States interests in the Pacific Basin can grow during the next ten years. However, this does not mean that the United States will once again discover Asia. It means rather a restoration of the historical ties that the United States had previously with Asia. Since 1945, the United States has fought two wars in Asia, and Asian problems have been critical issues in five of the nine presidential elections that have been held. Hence American interests in Asia have continually formed one of the pillars of U.S. foreign policy. The real anomaly was the wane in American interest in Asia that occurred as an aftereffect of the Vietnam War. The Reagan administration, however, has given high priority to relations with Asia, and has succeeded in broadening its ties with China, Japan, and the ASEAN nations.

SPEECH BY SECRETARY OF STATE GEORGE SHULTZ ENTITLED "FOREIGN POLICY PROSPECTS"
(Los Angeles, 10/19/84)

The failure of the Soviet campaign to stop deployment of the NATO missiles is directly attributable to the solidarity of the alliance. The same may be said of the unprecedented success of the Williamsburg Summit in issuing the joint security declaration. On that occasion, Japan for the first time participated as a partner in deliberations on security issues. Cooperative efforts were made at the London Summit also, even outside of the field of economics. We have now reached a period in time when we should study ways of modernizing our conventional defense capabilities in order to raise the nuclear threshold and reduce our dependence on nuclear weapons.

We have developed new relations with our friends in Asia, and have begun building a network of relations that will become one of the most important pillars supporting world prosperity and further development in the next century. It has only taken the United States ten short years since the Vietnam War to restore its position in Asia. Our allies in East Asia are very strong, and the outlook for continued good relations with them is bright.

During the past four years, U.S. trade with the Asian-Pacific region has grown larger, and at a faster rate, than U.S. trade with any other region.

With Japan, we have made progress toward solving our difficult economic problems. The primary reason for that progress is the mutual awareness of the political importance of the partnership between the two nations.

America's relations with Asia are not being strengthened at the expense of its relations with Europe or with Central and South

America. Relations with Asia do, however, present unique and attractive possibilities for the future. The free economic systems of East and Southeast Asia should serve as models for other developing nations.

There is today a growing concept of a Pacific community that contains within it the potential for increased cooperation among many nations of vastly diverse cultures, races, and political systems. This community is not institutionalized, in the way that our relationship with Europe is, but it does involve more consultation, attention to common interests, and an exhilarating vision of the future. We may be standing on the threshold of a brand new age of international relations in the Pacific region.

12

Traveling the Fifty States

During my five-year tour of duty as the Japanese Ambassador to the United States, from April 1980, to March 1985, I visited as many of the states as I could in an effort to learn first-hand what ordinary Americans thought about Japan, and what expectations they had of us Japanese. Fortunately I was able to visit all fifty states and Puerto Rico. I made speeches in all of these places, and was interviewed numerous times by local television stations. According to embassy records I made 218 of these speeches.

Each state has its own unique character, and I treasure fond memories from every one of my visits. Some of my experiences were particularly instructive in terms of future Japan-U.S. relations, however, and I want to describe a few of those here, in whatever order they come to mind. My own personal *interpretation* of America and of Japan-U.S. relations is evident in every chapter, of course, but in the vignettes that follow I will take even greater freedom in relating the more subjective impressions which everyday life in America made on me. Perhaps I should have entitled this chapter "Japan-U.S. Relations – A Backyard View."

Traveling about the United States, I was more than a few times impressed with how extensive the scope of Japanese activity had become. I would find Japanese people in the most unlikely places, completely acclimated and at home in the regional society. Among the Japanese I met were a woman who taught Japanese language in Reno, Nevada, and a professor of jazz in the music department at the Las Vegas campus of the University of Nevada. I came across a high-class hotel consultant operating in the Ozark resort region of Missouri, and an import-export specialist helping out

American businesses in Tampa, Florida. I met another fellow countryman teaching Japanese at a small college deep in the backcountry of Vermont, a Japanese physician giving pathology lectures at Tulane University in Louisiana, a Japanese dealer in precious jewelry in Omaha, Nebraska, and a Japanese breeder of eels in Virginia. Once in a rural town called Hagerstown, Maryland, near the West Virginia border, I encountered a Japanese housewife who spoke nostalgically of her memories of Tokyo. Japanese expatriates were to be seen everywhere, diligently engaged in some occupation or other.

The situation was much the same with Japanese students in America. I discovered young Japanese men and women studying in colleges and universities that most Japanese have never heard of — Clayton College in Omaha, Nebraska; Dakota State College in Madison, South Dakota; Vanderbilt University in Nashville, Tennessee; Florida Institute of Technology in Orlando, Florida; Lehigh University in Bethlehem, Pennsylvania — the list goes on and on. Seeing these Japanese students working to master English and sweating through courses in the specialized sciences, I was repeatedly amazed at the extent to which the activities of Japanese people in the United States had widened.

The question, however, is how these students are going to make the most of their experiences in America once they become working members of society. While I could visualize many of them playing useful roles as members of the growing "international set," I also felt that some were in danger of becoming a strange sort of hybrid that has no deep roots anywhere.

The number of persons of Japanese descent residing in the United States is said to be 750,000. From this number have come four members of Congress, namely Senators Daniel Inouye and Spark Matsunaga (both Democrats) from Hawaii, and Congressmen Norman Y. Mineta and Robert T. Matsui (both Democrats) of California. The number rises to five if we include S. I. Hayakawa, the former Senator from California.

George R. Ariyoshi, the Governor of Hawaii, is also of Japanese ancestry. This year, under Governor Ariyoshi, Hawaii is celebrating the 100th year of officially sanctioned immigration. These celebrations are all very significant.

The enthusiastic participation of Japanese-Americans in the

political arena is thus quite impressive. There seem to be few politically active younger Japanese-Americans preparing to take the place of those who have gone before, however, so one cannot be very optimistic about the future.

Persons of Japanese descent once accounted for more than half of Hawaii's population, but they now represent only about a third of the total. As a population grouping, therefore, their relative strength has declined.

Other prominent Japanese-Americans include the widely known Washington lobbyist and lawyer William Tanaka, and many doctors and dentists who have succeeded in private practice. In the business field, however, the number of influential Japanese is surprisingly small (although there are a few, such as Kei Sugawara who is involved in sea transport and other business ventures in New York). Quite a number in the Japanese-American community point to this fact as an indication of future problems.

Americans of Japanese descent who went through the bitter wartime experience of being forcibly uprooted from their homes and concentrated in Japanese camps are particularly sensitive to vicissitudes in Japan-U.S. relations. This sensitivity is based on a recurring fear that the economic and social structure that they have built up during the forty years since World War II will be once again ruined if Japan-U.S. trade friction becomes intense enough. This community is represented by the Japan-America Citizens League (JACL), which is participated in mainly by *nisei* (second generation) and *sansei* (third generation) Japanese-Americans. Mike Masaoka, a very prominent JACL leader, has been active since the war in improving Japan-U.S. relations, and he played a central role in founding the Japan-America Society in Washington. Another enthusiastic JACL member is William Hosokawa, honorary consul general of Japan in Denver and until recently the editor in chief of the *Denver Post*.

The primary objective of JACL is to demonstrate how commendably Americans of Japanese descent function in American society. The organization is deeply concerned about the impact that recent Japan-U.S. economic friction is having in the lives of Japanese-Americans. JACL has maintained a consistent policy of cooperating to localize and alleviate such friction as much as possible so that the problem does not deteriorate into an emotional Japan-U.S. confrontation. The league's relations with

138

Japan's embassy and consulates general have become much closer than they were formerly.

Toyoko Yamazaki has written poignantly of the harsh experiences suffered by the Japanese nisei in her novel *Futatsu no Sokoku* (*Two Homelands*). When a television dramatization of this novel — entitled "Sanga Moyu (Mountains and Rivers Ablaze)" — was aired in Japan by NHK, members of JACL were very worried about what might happen if it were shown in the United States. They feared that the story, though fictional, might be interpreted as factual by American viewers in general, and create unhelpful misconceptions about Japanese-Americans after the latter had worked so hard to be recognized as first-class U.S. citizens.

JACL sponsors a nationwide conference twice every year. At the Los Angeles conference held in 1982, the Subcommittee on Japan-U.S. Problems was formed as a subordinate organizational unit. I think this is one concrete manifestation of the concern that Japanese-Americans have in this area.

When making official trips throughout the United States, I tried to visit as many factories operated by Japanese companies in the area as time would permit. Many of these factories were in Massachusetts, Ohio, Pennsylvania, Georgia, Florida, Tennessee, Alabama, Arkansas, Texas, and California. Management practices differ from industry to industry, but, in general, the number of Japanese staffers was extremely small, and managerial responsibility was widely delegated to Americans. It seems to be a universal practice among these companies to put labor management entirely in American hands.

Except for the engineers who were on hand to provide technical guidance, most of the Japanese personnel were found in charge of accounting or overseas transactions. Americans were handling just about everything else, and turning out good results.

Japanese managers had been very anxious to find out whether or not the so-called Japanese management methods would prove effective with American workers employed on American soil. The unanimous consent among these managers at the factories I visited was that those methods were working splendidly, producing results that were satisfactory in terms of both product quality and productivity.

139

One of the keys to this success seems to be the sophisticated programs that have been set up for the American supervisory personnel. Key supervisors and foremen are invited to attend practical training courses in Japan. The skills and production techniques learned in there are then put to use back in the U.S. factory.

I was also impressed by the way in which very careful attention is given to labor management in all of the factories I visited. This task is being accomplished relatively smoothly by using American labor managers.

Management practices differ widely between the factories in the North, where unionization is legally required, and those in the South, where such is not the case.

Union activity is entrenched in some industries due to the strong influence of the United Auto Workers (UAW), the International Brotherhood of Electrical Workers, and other powerful unions. Other industries have not unionized — even though they do not ban union activity — because the majority of their employees do not wish to.

How best to manage labor relations will continue to be a very major concern of Japanese companies operating in the United States. I hope that new entrants into this group will follow the good example of those who have preceded them in establishing wholesome labor-management relations.

Another thing that impressed me was the all-out effort that many Japanese companies have made in cooperating with local residents on community projects. Americans are very active in volunteer and charity work. It is essential for businesses operating in American society, therefore, to cooperate enthusiastically in these activities. If a company takes the attitude that profits are all that matters, it will tend to neglect its societal obligations to the local community. This invariably leads to local opposition that eventually affects the company's operations.

I am reminded here of the somewhat humorous story of a Sanyo Electric subsidiary in Arkansas. The company decided to sponsor a Japanese-style athletic festival, only to have it become a popular regular event for which the whole town turns out. This story was enthusiastically told and retold by Arkansas Governor Bill Clinton as well as by the local mayor.

Every year in Macon, Georgia, toward the end of March, a big cherry blossom festival is held, highlighted by a crowd-drawing parade that features members of Congress, state legislators, local mayors, and the president of Mercer University, among other dignitaries. This annual event has now become even more magnificent through the generous support given by the YKK zipper factory which is located in Macon. Such community involvement is highly valued in the United States.

Following the end of World War II, while Japan was still under occupation, the United States instituted the GARIOA (Government Account for Relief in Occupied Areas) program under which many Japanese — both those in leadership careers and young people in general — were sent to the United States to study and to learn about America. The main objective was to develop a human resource pool that could be drawn from in the future. I myself studied in the United States under the GARIOA program in 1951 and 1952. This experience was a great benefit to me in my subsequent career as a diplomat.

The GARIOA program was further expanded through the Fulbright Exchange Program — still very active today — which was originally proposed by former Senator William Fulbright of Arkansas. Some 5,800 Japanese students have now studied in the United States through the Fulbright program. Under the same program, a considerable number of students and professors have come from the United States to Japan, to study and to lecture, respectively. The Fulbright program has played a tremendous role in Japan's postwar development.

In April 1984, the GARIOA-Fulbright Alumni Association (chaired by Daisuke Yamauchi, president of Mainichi Shimbunsha), with the cooperation of the United States Information Service (USIS), sponsored a tour of the United States to commemorate the 30th anniversary of the Fulbright program. About 100 people participated in this "sentimental journey" including tour leader Yamauchi, assistant tour leader Hachiro Oyama (chairman of Johnson Wax of Japan), and a number of wives. After visiting Washington, D.C., together, the group split up so that each alumnus could visit his U.S. alma mater and share happy reunions with former classmates.

While in Washington, the group was invited to many festivities, including a warm reception by Vice President Bush at the White House and a luncheon in the Senate dining room organized by

Senator Matsunaga. I was one of the participants in these alumni festivities, which were very moving. I also invited the group to come to the ambassador's residence, just before the annual reception to celebrate the Emperor's Birthday. This informal meeting was all too short, but we had a good time sharing with one another our memories of student days in the United States.

Senator Fulbright, the founder of the Fulbright program, was defeated in a subsequent reelection bid and now practices law in a Washington law office. Whenever we meet he tends to wax somewhat sentimental. "I am always greatly moved to see how this program—the idea for which came from my own experience as a Rhodes scholar in England—has flowered and born much fruit," the former Senator will say. "Many countries have benefited from this program, but the country which has been most enthusiastic in expressing its appreciation, and which has produced the best results, is Japan."

In 1979, William Fulbright visited Japan at the invitation of Japanese Fulbright students and was granted an honorary doctor of laws degree by Waseda University. I will never forget how deeply moved the Senator was by this token of Japanese appreciation.

Besides its headquarters in Tokyo, the Fulbright Alumni Association of Japan has nine branch chapters in such cities as Osaka, Nagoya, and Fukuoka. By organizing golf tournaments and other fund-raising activities, the association is able to invite nearly twenty American students to come to Japan each year.

William Fulbright is from Fayetteville, Arkansas. To honor the former Senator, the University of Arkansas established the Fulbright Institute of International Relations, of which I am now a trustee. One would not have expected Arkansas to be all that taken up with international problems, but the university is doing its best to live up to the fine tradition established by its illustrious Senator.

Senator Fulbright is also known as an avid golfer. The following anecdote is often told at the Burning Tree Club, just outside Washington, D.C., where Fulbright is an active member.

The story involves a bet that the Senator made with an opponent who was sure to beat him. Fulbright showed up on the first tee with his left hand wrapped in a bandage. Saddened by the look of pain on the Senator's face, the opponent proposed terms that were more lenient than usual. Fulbright accepted these terms and seemed greatly relieved. Then he pulled off the bandage, tossed it aside, and began flourishing his driver without cracking a smile. This episode permanently established Fulbright's prowess at his club as a most formidable negotiator.

Burning Tree is also well known in Japan as the course where Prime Minister Nobosuke Kishi played with President Dwight Eisenhower in 1956. Kishi's partner was Koichiro Asakai, Japan's Ambassador to the United States at the time. Eisenhower's partner was Senator Prescott Bush, father of the current vice president.

In one commemorative photograph, Ike is seen raising both arms overhead in the "banzai" pose familiar to Japanese. Asakai recollects the occasion and gives the following explanation. When the two sides were being introduced to each other, Ike gestured toward Bush and said "This is Prescott Bush, a good old Harvard man." Actually a graduate of Yale, Bush protested to Ike, "Do you think I graduated from such a hicktown university?" Taken aback, Ike then said "I surrender!" and raised his hands over his head. Whether this was an expression of the intense rivalry between Harvard and Yale, or merely of love to one's alma mater, this story told by former ambassador Asakai gives one a little taste of Ivy League school spirit.

Vice President George Bush also went to Yale, incidentally, where he played third base and captained the baseball team. He is now an avid tennis buff, and when he can get away enjoys playing against family members at his ocean front summer home in Kennebunkport, Maine. Once in a while, however, he is also seen playing golf at Burning Tree, where he is known for his herculean tee shots.

Besides the Fulbright Research Institute, another facility that impressed me a great deal is The Maureen and Mike Mansfield Library located at the University of Montana in Missoula, Montana, named for the current U.S. Ambassador to Japan who taught at the university as a young man. Preserved in one room of this library are many photographs and other memorabilia which recall Mansfield's active public life. The items on display include official documents that were signed during Mansfield's tenure as Democratic floor leader in the Senate.

It is reported that the University of Montana is also planning to broaden its curriculum in the area of Japan-U.S. research in order to commemorate Mike Mansfield's contributions while ambassador to better Japan-U.S. relations.

The late Kazushige Hirasawa, who served in the Foreign Ministry before World War II, became quite popular after the war as a radio and TV commentator on international affairs for NHK, Japan's national broadcasting corporation. Earlier in his career, before the War, faced with the selection of an American college at which to undertake part of his training as a junior diplomat, Hirasawa chose Bates College in remote Lewiston, Maine, where he knew he would not find another Japanese. There he was a member of the debating team, together with his longtime friend Edmund Muskie, the former senator and President Jimmy Carter's Secretary of State. When a proposal was made to establish the Hirasawa Memorial Lectures on Japan-U.S. relations at Bates, interested Japanese raised about ¥ 100 million toward the project through public solicitations. A presentation ceremony was conducted at the college on October 11, 1984, attended by Hirasawa's widow Asako. It is very moving to find such keen interest in international exchange programs at regional U.S. colleges like Bates, which are almost totally unknown in Japan.

When considering international exchange, one must not overlook the activities of sister cities. As of April 1985, there are 176 pairs of sister-cities, and nine sister-prefecture/state combinations, for a total of 185 sister relationships between Japan and the United States.

In the United States, the American Sister-City Association has its headquarters in Washington, D.C. A national convention is held every summer in an appropriate city. Foreign dignitaries are invited to this convention, where the significance of the sister-city relationships is thoroughly discussed.

I was invited to participate in the 1981 convention held in Kansas City, and made a speech at the 1983 convention in Phoenix, Arizona. I was very impressed with the enthusiasm shown by the participants from cities all across the United States.

These sister-city affiliations deserve special mention because they facilitate international exchange and dialogue, and contribute toward better mutual understanding between Japan and the United States at the regional grassroots level.

We need to promote more of these grassroot level exchanges — between mayors and other city and state officials on the one hand, and between school students on the other — in order to avoid needless misunderstandings and to be able to see things from the other's point of view.

In the interest of further strengthening the ties between Japan and the United States, it is to be hoped that such sister-city involvement will become increasingly active.

When Prime Minister Suzuki visited the United States in May 1981, it was agreed that the Japanese Government would contribute $250,000 a year to Youth For Understanding (YFU) in order to promote more exchanges between Japanese and American young people. This policy was actually implemented through the Japan-U.S. Senate Scholarship Program.

Under this program, each of the fifty U.S. Senators recommends two high school students from his or her state. Each of these 100 students selected then spends eight weeks in Japan each summer, living with a Japanese family and learning about the country firsthand. All of the paperwork is handled by a YFU office located in Washington, D.C. YFU is one of the two large international youth organizations currently operating in the United States, the other being American Field Service (AFS). Both are supported out of State Department funds.

The special exchange program was put into operation in 1982. Before departing for Japan, all of the students gather in Washington to facilitate YFU coordination as well as a thorough orientation by State Department officials. They also attend a reception held in their honor by the Japanese ambassador.

After returning to the United States from Japan, many of these high school students sent letters to the embassy, praising Japan's natural beauty, the courteousness and cleanliness of the Japanese people, and the warmth of Japanese homes. Some students added that they wish to see these commendable Japanese qualities adopted into American home and social life. All wrote to express their appreciation, while stressing how enjoyable and meaningful their stay was, and how their eyes were opened to a whole new world. When we at the embassy saw how appreciatively Japan's cooperation in this plan was received, and realized that good seed was being planted for future harvests, we felt very gratified.

Subsequently, a program was initiated under which students from Japan's 46 prefectures visit the United States every year for 12 months. Thus high school students — who tend to be very impressionable — from both nations are now exposed to the national and individual traits of the other country through the intimate experience of family life. This experience leads to the formation of deep personal ties that transcend culture. I think this is extremely significant for the future of Japan-U.S. relations, and it is my ardent wish that such programs as this become even more effective.

There was one student letter in particular that really impressed me. The writer reflected on the fact that his group, after gathering in Washington for the pre-departure orientation, then separated never to meet again. He went on to say that he thought the Japan experiences could be made even more beneficial if the group were to meet once more after returning so that students could share with one another what they had learned, what impressions they had received, and what attitudes they were having to reevaluate.

It is a pity that this high school student's wish cannot be realized. There are regional post-return programs for some of the students, but the expense of gathering them all together once more is, unfortunately, prohibitive.

In a similar vein, there are high school social studies teacher invitation programs that are administered by the Ministry of Foreign Affairs, the Japan Foundation, and the Keidanren Information Center, respectively. The aim of these programs is to bring American social studies teachers to Japan so that they may better understand Japan as it really is. The ultimate goal is that American junior-high and high school social studies teachers will impart to their students correct views of Japan instead of the old stereotypes that are so negatively biased and misleading. An alumni organization is now being formed for instructors who have visited Japan under these programs. I believe this is very significant in terms of the positive impact it will have on future generations.

Turning to the area of cooperation oriented toward regional society, a program was started about three years ago for inviting five Washington, D.C., school personnel to Japan each year. This

146

program is based on private contributions, and is promoted by the Japan Chamber of Commerce and Industry (*Shokokai*) and Japan Press Club. With the support of the Embassy this program was originally conceived as a tangible expression of Japanese gratitude for the kind consideration and help given by school officials in Washington, D.C., and surrounding districts to the education of the children of Japanese citizens residing in the Washington area.

A similar program has been carried on for many years, and with very good results, by Japanese citizens residing in the Los Angeles area. These programs will probably be expanded across the United States as the number of Japanese residents increases in various localities.

Washington, D.C., is a town of politics and politicians, the center of both federal-government and congressional activity in America. Not surprisingly, the city attracts multitudes of representatives of interest groups and private companies from all over the United States and indeed the world.

Looking at membership lists for such prominent social clubs as the Metropolitan Club, the F Street Club, and the Cosmos Club, one finds many names of Washington-based executives of major corporations and numerous representatives of influential industrial organizations.

Lobbying has developed into a unique and powerful institution in American politics, and the number of lobbyists operating in Washington is growing steadily year after year.

Such well-known streets in Washington as Connecticut Avenue, K Street, and 19th Street are lined with fine restaurants which do a brisk lunch and dinner business. The sharp increase in the number of these fancy restaurants (which were nowhere to be seen just ten or twenty years ago) is partly attributable to the growth in lobbyist activity.

There are said to be some 45,000 lawyers in Washington, which is more than twice the number of all Japanese lawyers put together. This reflects the fact that the city is the center of congressional activity as well as the seat of the federal government. One American wit advocated resolving the problem of Japan-U.S. economic friction by permanently exiling all Washington lawyers to Japan.

The political activity of lobbying is quite foreign to most

Japanese and one in which they are uncomfortable. This notwithstanding, the Japanese are now beginning to more fully appreciate the importance of lobbying operations. Some of the larger Japanese corporations now carry on lobbying efforts through their own duly registered Washington representatives and are starting to see these efforts rewarded.

Surveying the situation that has prevailed until now, it can be said that professional Washington lobbyists have made a lucrative business of representing Japanese business interests. In some cases Japanese companies have been duped into paying exorbitant fees for bogus or otherwise ineffective lobbying action.

Many prominent lobbyists were formerly in high government positions. A few of these, after making a name for themselves as harsh Japan critics during their government tenure, then did an about-face and started drawing high salaries as lobbyists for Japanese corporations.

I think that the best route for Japanese companies to follow is first to gain a thorough knowledge of lobbying procedures in the United States, and then to study ways to use these procedures most effectively. This will enable them to carry on lobbying efforts most fruitfully in their own behalf.

There are many social clubs in Washington. The most prominent are the Metropolitan, Cosmos, International, University, Federal, F Street, Georgetown, and Congressional clubs, but the list goes on and on. It is at these clubs that much of Washington's active social life is played out.

Among the foremost clubs, the Metropolitan and the Cosmos are said to boast the most prestigious pedigrees. In the Metropolitan Club, to which I belonged, there is a relatively high percentage of lawyers, and its membership is also known to include many power brokers who wield tremendous influence in the government and the Washington bureaucracy.

Membership at the Cosmos Club is tilted more toward scholars and intellectuals. The club is proud of the more than one dozen Nobel Prize laureates whom it counts among its members.

"The Cosmos Club has a lot of brains, but not a whole lot of money," said one fellow Metropolitan member to me with a knowing wink. "By comparison, our club excels in both intellectual and financial resources."

148

The most highly pedigreed clubs do not recognize female membership. The Metropolitan Club does not permit any women to enter it during the daytime. Members may be accompanied by their wives only after dark. At the Cosmos Club, females are not allowed to come in the front door, and must use a side entrance. Such practices are commonly observed at private social clubs throughout the United States.

As the feminine answer to these exclusive male clubs, the Sulgrave Club has an all-female membership and only allows men to enter when accompanied by a member.

The F Street Club is renowned both for the quality of its membership and the excellence of its cuisine.

Not to be confused with these downtown social clubs are the exclusive country clubs also to be found in Washington. The latter include such famous clubs as Chevy Chase, Burning Tree, Congressional, Kenwood, and Columbia.

The Burning Tree Country Club is famous in Japan for hosting the golf match between Ike and Kishi. This club is also known for its policy of limiting play to males only. This club is rumored to have been created in 1923 by a group of male players who were fed up with slow playing women golfers. They decided to build a course where they could play at their own pace. This club still strictly enforces the rules prohibiting women from coming inside the gate. During the hottest part of the summer, some members play with their shirts off.

A woman recently filed suit against these clubs in a Maryland court, alleging that club practices were contemptuous of women. Since then, the possible ramifications of this court action are a frequent topic of discussion among golfers.

These Washington country clubs are currently recognized as natural environmental preserves, and as such enjoy special immunities to taxes on their fixed assets. Depending on the outcome of the pending court case in Maryland, however, the clubs may be faced with a decision, namely to either pay the fixed asset taxes levied by the state and perpetuate their male paradises, or open their doors to women and continue to enjoy the tax immunities.

Washington also has social clubs for its prominent women, namely the International Club and the International Neighbors Club. Wives of cabinet members, wives of Congressmen, and other noted women join one or the other of these clubs according to their fancy. Wives of foreign ambassadors are also invited to join. Membership in both clubs is not permitted, and there seems to be some competition between them in soliciting a prominent woman to join.

One characteristic of Americans is their love for speeches and debates. Every major U.S. city has its Rotary Club, Lions Club, and Kiwanis Club as well as its forums for discussing world trends and foreign affairs. These institutions invite speakers to give lectures on politics, economics, or international problems. These talks are usually followed by a vigorous debate on the issues discussed.

Among such institutions that enjoy national prestige in the United States are the Commonwealth Club in San Francisco, the Mid-Atlantic Club in Chicago, the Council on Foreign Affairs in New York, the Economic Club in Detroit, and the Houston Forum in Houston. It is considered a great honor to be invited to speak at one of these clubs, and the invitations are much prized.

The usual format is to speak for 30 to 40 minutes, then respond to questions for another 30 to 40 minutes. Once the questioning starts, the participating members raise their hands and vie to be recognized. When given the floor, they succinctly state their own views and press the speaker on any doubtful points. It is often difficult for the moderator to keep track of all the hands that are going up and to give everyone a fair chance to participate. This contrasts sharply with the tamer *koenkai* which is the closest Japanese counterpart of these meetings.

The National Press Club in Washington, D.C., invites prominent figures in America and around the world to speak at its functions, and is hence well known far beyond the environs of Washington and the shores of the United States. It was at this press club, in November 1969, that Prime Minister Eisaku Sato stated that "in the unlikely event that the Republic of Korea should be attacked militarily, Japan will positively and promptly determine its position in response to prior consultation by the U.S." It was also here that Prime Minister Suzuki, in May 1981, said "The U.S. Seventh fleet has been redeployed to the Indian Ocean, leaving the seas around Japan untended. It is only natural that Japan should protect its own home waters." During

150

this same speech Suzuki clearly set forth the geographical scope of Japanese self-defense, namely "the waters around Japan out to several hundred nautical miles, and the sea lanes out to 1,000 nautical miles." This was the first open declaration of this Japanese policy to the outside world.

During these club functions, at which lunch is served, those attending may write questions on forms provided for that purpose. The forms are collected and the moderator selects from them several questions which he or she poses to the speaker. The National Press Club has become famous for the mordant severity of these questions, which are often very tough for the speaker to answer. It is traditional for the final question to be on the light side, and how wittily the speaker responds to it is said to determine his or her future reputation as a speechmaker. These occasions provide a good opportunity for the gifted speaker to shine, but they can be very treacherous for the unwary.

America has what to Japanese thinking is an excessive number of unbelievably wealthy individuals. Take for example the business executives who fly into Washington from Detroit or Chicago in their private jets just to have lunch with someone or attend a dinner party. They think no more of these little excursions than a Japanese executive would of riding for an hour or so in his car to keep a dinner engagement.

Another surprise is the large number of wealthy people who live quite vigorous but rather spartan private lives with very few frills. They enjoy their holidays and vacations to the hilt, but ordinarily sit down to very simple meals. Some wealthy wives show astonishingly little interest in lavish attire or the latest fashions. When we Japanese meet these rich Americans on the golf course, we find that their bags and clubs have already seen many seasons. I have observed a lot of extremely wealthy Americans using clubs that are ten or fifteen years old. This would be unthinkable in Japan.

Americans in general have a very strong interest in charitable activities. I am always impressed with their willingness to participate in a worthy cause. Wealthy people are naturally expected to contribute generously, but the magnitude of their giving—to their alma maters and to charitable social institutions—is truly enviable. The tax write-offs are said to be a large factor in this liberality, but it is still American generosity that makes it happen.

151

Walter Annenberg, who owns the high-circulation magazine *TV Guide,* is a man of tremendous personal wealth and has served as the U.S. Ambassador to the U.K. for five years during the Nixon-Ford administration. During the early period of the Reagan administration Annenberg's wife Lee served as the Director of Protocol at the State Department. The Annenberg's home in Palm Springs, California, is also famous for being the place where President and Mrs. Reagan spend their Christmas vacations.

My wife and I were invited to this fabulous home as we were returning to Japan, and spent two days there. It takes five or six minutes by car to get from the front gate to the mansion itself, where one is greeted by a lavish display of marble. Inside, the walls are literally covered with original paintings by such French impressionists as Monet and Degas. The pool and the tennis courts are such as a visitor might expect, but there is also an expansive golf course from which one looks off in the distance to the mountains. I felt that I was in a well-kept garden — not only on the greens but in the fairways as well — and was even reluctant to take out a divot.

The contrast between the United States and Japan is very sharp, both in terms of the scale of private wealth, and in the manner in which truly wealthy Americans exercise reserve and emphasize utility in their approach to private life.

13

Homogeneity and Heterogeneity

The language of the political communiqué that resulted from the Bonn Summit contains references to three ideals that represent common values binding the advanced Western nations together, namely *freedom, democracy,* and *human rights.*

With this in mind, I was led to reflect on recent Japan-U.S. relations and to take another look at the joint communiqué and press releases that were issued after the Japan-U.S. summit meeting. In the joint statement issued by Suzuki and Reagan in May 1981 the following passage occurs: "The Prime Minister and the President, recognizing that the alliance between Japan and the United States is built upon the mutually held values of democracy and freedom, have reaffirmed the solidarity, friendship, and mutual trust that obtain between these two nations." In November 1983, President Reagan visited Japan and met with Prime Minister Nakasone. In a press release following this meeting, Nakasone stated that "these two nations, which share in common the values of freedom and democracy, have an obligation to cooperate in the interest of world peace and prosperity." Reagan made a similar statement in his press release after the historic meeting. What is evident in all of these statements is an awareness that the Japan-U.S. alliance has been developed on the basis of commonly held ideals, or what we might term *value homogeneity* (see appendix 5).

Since fighting its war for independence 200 years ago, Americans have valued *freedom* (*liberty*) more than any other ideal. The cracked Liberty Bell is preserved at Independence Hall in Philadelphia as a symbol of the joy of the newly conceived nation, while the Statue of Liberty rises majestically at the entrance to New York's harbor. Upon sighting this great symbol of hope, the emigrants who crossed the Atlantic from Europe are said to have felt that they had finally reached the land of freedom. This statue, known affectionately as "the lady" by New Yorkers, was presented by France to commemorate the first centennial of American independence. One hundred years later, after the ravages of time have taken their toll on the statue, a plan is being promoted in America and France to finance badly needed repairs from privately donated funds.

Japan has its own history of struggling for the ideal of freedom. Her struggle began with the movement for a free citizenry during the Meiji era, continued through the hopeful period of "Taisho democracy" following World War I and into the 1920s, and finally culminated in the strong national commitment to freedom which has become deeply rooted in post-war Japan. It is no accident that the long political reign of the Liberal Democratic Party in post-war Japan has coincided with this era of Japanese history which is characterized by such a high regard for liberty.

The United States and Japan also share a common basic political system, namely democracy. There are differences of course between the Japanese parliamentary system and the American presidential system with its separate executive branch; but the fundamental underlying values of freedom and democracy are the same, and form a solid basis for the Japan-U.S. alliance.

In the context of the debates raging over recent Japan-U.S. trade friction, however, Americans have recently leveled strong criticism against Japan's national bureaucracy and distribution system. From a Japanese perspective, these systems — whatever their ultimate merits or demerits — are part of the very fabric of life in Japan, and seeing them scathingly criticized strikes a sensitive nerve. That is why some commentators in Japan have argued that the so-called *economic* or *trade* friction might more properly be termed *cultural* friction. If we take this argument to one logical conclusion, we could say that Japan and the United States are after all heterogeneous entities with disparate histories and cultures, and that therefore we cannot hope to find adequate common ground on which to build a meaningful alliance.

However, there is no reason why differences in history, culture, or tradition should pose any fundamental barrier to the creation of a sound alliance. Japan and the United States do speak different languages and have different historical and cultural heritages, but by sharing common ideals of freedom and democracy, our two nations have forged a viable alliance under which our mutual disparities may be subsumed. It is quite true that an alliance is not something that will flourish of its own accord if neglected. It must be constantly watered, weeded, and cultivated, lest it wither and die. By the same token, Japan and America cannot take each other for granted if they wish to make their alliance prosper; they must build on the homogeneity that binds the two countries together.

The idea that Japan is a democratic nation is now fairly well established in the American consciousness. A letter sent to me from a congressman was addressed to the "Ambassador of the Republic of Japan," and once I was slightly embarrassed when a Senator introduced me by the same title in a Japanese exhibit room at a museum. Perhaps those who made these faux pas merely assumed that since Japan is a democracy it must also be a republic like the United States.

Many of the promotional materials prepared by the Japanese Embassy for distribution in the United States have emphasized that these two nations, for all the disparity between their cultural backgrounds, have nevertheless been able to strengthen their cooperative relationship, and that they will continue to do so.

Japanese food has become extremely popular in the United States. This has happened despite the fact that Japanese cuisine is somewhat alien to conventional American tastes. Americans invited to dinner parties given at the ambassador's residence came with high expectations that they would be served Japanese dishes. They came prepared to test their palates on real Japanese food, and having been given the opportunity to do so, they went away satisfied and happy.

Another interesting phenomenon is the intense interest among Americans in the Kabuki and Noh dramas. These traditional Japanese art forms are altogether unlike anything found in Western art, and yet Americans have demonstrated a keen appreciation for them.

The world of Kabuki, for example, is utterly foreign to American society, and yet a cultural environment is developing in the United States in which a real appreciation for Kabuki can be nurtured. This development is based not on a superficial craving for something new and exotic, but on a deeper and more basic receptivity to good art.

155

When the Daikabuki Ichiza troupe visited the United States three years ago, Nakamura Utaemon [family name given first] played the leading role in *Sumidagawa* (Sumida River), a play that is difficult even for Japanese audiences to assimilate. But Americans who saw it were entranced by the sheer power of Utaemon's art, and liked this play better than any of the others that were performed, even though the others were easier to understand and offered more beautiful costumes and props. This is one example of heterogeneous culture actually working to strengthen Japan-U.S. relations.

Incidentally, I had a similar experience regarding Utaemon's *Sumidagawa* several years ago in Australia, where I was stationed previously. I secretly feared that Australians would not be able to relate to the performance, but this turned out to be a needless worry. In Sydney, Melbourne, and Adelaide, wherever the refined art of this "national human treasure" Utaemon was performed, the Australians were profoundly moved.

Performances by the Ondehko traditional drummers of Sado have recently been enthusiastically received all around the United States. Although their style is foreign to the modern American audience, their powerful rolling drum beats seem to call forth a basic response to rhythm that is common to all people.

As long as certain fundamental attitudes are held in common, diverse traditions and cultures can work side by side without causing conflict. This diversity can in fact work to strengthen cross-cultural relationships. In terms of a simple schoolroom analogy, it is like the strong individual personalities who are most appreciated by their classmates.

Japan has been called the faceless society. Her army of businessmen work from dawn to dusk, practically indistinguishable in their almost identical dark suits. They carry on tidy stereotypical existences as though pressed out of the same mold. And what impression do they make when they go abroad? Look at them there, assembling in front of the tour guide who is holding up the little flag. They do everything together, according to plan, rarely speaking to anyone outside their group. They descend upon some famous place like a flock of Asian geese, look about for a while, and suddenly fly away in the same manner as they came. To the local population, these Japanese tourists seem to be devoid of individual personality. To many they seem downright peculiar.

The traditional stereotype is changing, however, and Japan is beginning to show its face. I think we may interpret this as a clear indication of the changing American attitudes toward Japan. In the collective American consciousness, Japan is finally being accepted as a legitimate member of the same team.

Appendix 5

Cited below are several important recent instances in which particular stress was given to the ideals held in common between Japan and the United States, in the context of Western solidarity.

SUZUKI-REAGAN JOINT COMMUNIQUÉ (May 8, 1981)

"President Reagan and Prime Minister Suzuki met in Washington on May 7 and 8 for a comprehensive and fruitful review of the current international situation and U.S.-Japan relationship. They pledged that they would work closely together in pursuit of world peace and prosperity. The President and the Prime Minister, recognizing that the alliance between the United States and Japan is built upon their shared values of democracy and liberty, reaffirmed their solidarity, friendship and mutual trust."

WILLIAMSBURG DECLARATION ON ECONOMIC RECOVERY (May 30, 1983)

"Our nations are united in their dedication to democracy, individual freedom, creativity, moral purpose, human dignity, and personal and cultural development. It is to preserve, sustain, and extend these shared values that our prosperity is important."

ANNOUNCEMENT BY PRIME MINISTER NAKASONE AT CONCLUSION OF JAPAN-U.S. SUMMIT TALKS (November 10, 1983)

"Yesterday and today, the President and I had very productive meetings covering a wide range of subjects. Through these meetings, we reconfirmed the importance for Japan and the United States, two countries sharing the common ideas and values of freedom and democracy of promoting further cooperation toward peace and prosperity of the world."

ANNOUNCEMENT BY PRESIDENT REAGAN
(November 10, 1983)

"Japan and America are bound by shared values of freedom, democracy, and peace. We're committed to greater future cooperation across a broad spectrum of political, economic, security, educational, cultural, and scientific affairs."

POLITICAL DECLARATION ON 40TH ANNIVERSARY OF END OF WORLD WAR II (May 3, 1985)

"Having put behind us the antagonisms that once divided us, we have now begun to move toward reconciliation and cooperation in the name of commonly held values. Today we are bound together by an unshakable and permanent friendship in which peace abounds. In our nations, the principles of freedom and democracy are held in common, as is our resolve to safeguard human rights." (Source: *Sekai no Ugoki,* Special Issue on Bonn Summit, Sekai no Ugokisha, p. 36)

14

The Future:

A Dialog Between
Ambassador Yoshio Okawara and
Tokyo Professor Nagayo Homma

Homma Ambassador, you were in Washington from April 1980, until mid-March of this year — a period of five years. In terms of U.S. administrations, this period extends from the height of the Iran hostage crisis in the last year of the Carter administration, through President Reagan's entire first administration and into the early months of his second. I think you will agree that there were many significant and even disturbing developments during this period, both for Japan-U.S. relations and for the American economy and domestic politics.

Okawara Yes, it gave me a good opportunity to directly experience the differences between the Carter and Reagan administrations. When I went to Washington in 1980, Americans everywhere were extremely disturbed over the hostage situation, and many were very concerned about how Japan would handle its relations with Iran.

Homma Jimmy Carter was a newcomer to Washington, and there were a lot of reservations about his leadership ability. The hostage crisis further eroded public trust in that ability. Did this make President Reagan's leadership style seem all the more forceful?

Okawara Yes, I think that is true in the sense that the ascendancy of Ronald Reagan is closely connected with the desire of the American people for something new and different.

Homma The administration passed from the Democrats to the Republicans, and the latter were successful in their reelection bid in 1984. Reagan's reelection is in fact the first time such a bid has gone smoothly since Eisenhower was reelected in

1956.* Except for the four years of the Carter administration, moreover, the Republicans have controlled the White House ever since President Johnson decided not to run for a second term. So, Ambassador, you were in Washington during a rather unusual period in recent American political history.

Okawara In the waning months of the Carter presidency, there was a kind of gloom hanging over America. In part this was due to the economy, which was in very bad shape, with both inflation and unemployment on the rise.

It was during the Carter administration that the second oil shock occurred. In some ways I think this second shock hit America even harder than the first one did. Perhaps that is one way in which the impacts of the first and second oil shocks on Japan and the United States can be contrasted.

The first oil shock dealt Japan a very damaging blow. As a consequence, however, Japan was better prepared for the second one and handled it very adroitly.

The first oil shock did make a big impact in America too, but America, compared to Japan, had a much greater capacity to absorb the blow. When the second shock hit, however, the United States had largely exhausted its absorbing ability, and the economy was hurt very badly. The wholesale shift away from large automobiles to compacts was, I think, a direct effect of the second oil shock.

The U.S. economy was already in bad shape when I first took up my duties in Washington, and the future looked even gloomier. In the Iran hostage debacle Americans felt that they were being dragged around by the nose. To be thus humbled by a country with Iran's limited resources was a great international embarrassment. And the worst part was the feeling of utter frustration and helplessness. The American people were disappointed in the Carter presidency, and I think their frustrations with that administration led to the defeat of the incumbent in November 1980 and the consequent victory of the Republican candidate, Ronald Reagan.

But doubts as to President Carter's leadership ability had

---

*Translator's Note: Richard M. Nixon's 1972 reelection bid was also very successful.

also begun to surface internationally. Some national leaders, particularly in Western Europe, were beginning to question whether Jimmy Carter could really carry his own weight among them.

Homma In Japan too, I think there was real concern over the potential instability and dangers inherent in the U.S. presidential election system itself. Then Ronald Reagan came along with his stronger brand of presidential leadership. In some ways President Reagan resembles Franklin D. Roosevelt, who was first inaugurated in 1933. FDR was also elected during a bleak time of economic stagnation, following a great financial panic. He told the American people, in so many words, that they should persevere because his administration was marching ahead of them. He changed the mood of the country. Ronald Reagan seems — in terms of sentiment and mood — to be modeling his leadership style after FDR's.

Okawara Indeed, President Reagan often invokes the name of Franklin Roosevelt. Reagan formerly was a Democrat himself, and makes no bones about his deep personal esteem for FDR.

Homma So the Reagan people seemed to have this idea that they were going to dramatically change the mood of the country. And in fact, in 1981, during the first year of Reagan's first term, they did indeed breathe new life into Washington's political atmosphere. They had an open agenda of new optimistic policies, with which they rekindled American hopes and dreams. People were saying "Let's see what this fellow can do."

Okawara The most impressive development during my five-year tour in Washington was the way in which America, during four years of Reagan's presidency, completely recovered the national confidence that it lost during the Carter years. Reagan restored to Americans their strong national pride and revitalized their deeply ingrained patriotism. I think this is one reason for Reagan's tremendous popularity.

Homma I suppose the greatest concern at the embassy in Washington was what kind of Japan policy the Reagan administration would pursue.

Okawara Before we get into that, there is another thing which should be mentioned. When Foreign Minister Okita and Secretary of State Vance met in Paris in December 1979 — which was before I was assigned to Washington — Japan was accused of being "altogether too insensitive" to American interests as regarding the Iran oil problem. And when I went to Washington shortly thereafter, I found a widespread feeling among Americans that retaliatory measures of some kind should be considered if Japan purchased Iranian oil.

No sooner did I get to Washington, however, than ABC invited me to be interviewed on one of their talk shows. I knew exactly what would happen once I was on live TV. They would throw everything they had at me, no holds barred. And yet, knowing that, I hated to take the easy way out. This was the first difficult decision I had to make after assuming my post in Washington.

I still had not presented my credentials formally to the United States government, and so, after much agonizing, I declined the interview, explaining to ABC that I couldn't speak in any official capacity as ambassador until my credentials were presented and accepted. Then mid-April rolled around, and the news was reported that Japan had decided not to buy Iranian oil after all. American public opinion was transformed overnight.

The truth of the matter is that the Japanese decision was a purely economic one. Iranian oil would not be purchased because it was priced too high, not because Japan sympathized with the excruciating U.S. dilemma over the hostages in Iran, and not because of any political decision to avoid acting against Washington's wishes. Nevertheless, the decision largely dispelled a lot of the prevalent anti-Japanese sentiment. The *New York Times* even carried an editorial entitled "Thanks, and Oil, to Japan."

I had been told that Americans are an emotional people, and that a single crisis or major news story could turn national sentiment on its ear. I certainly found this to be true in the case of the oil decision and its effect on American feelings toward Japan.

Homma This must have made you all the more anxious to learn how U.S. policy toward Japan would change with the new administration.

Okawara Ronald Reagan had been governor of California, and came to Japan in 1972 as President Nixon's special presidential envoy. As governor of California he had adopted a pro-Pacific and pro-Asia policy. The knowledge of these facts was rather reassuring.

In addition, General Alexander Haig — with whom I had some personal acquaintance when he served as a White House aide under President Nixon — had been appointed Secretary of State. This also made me feel more warmly disposed toward the new administration.

Haig was at that time the president of United Technologies Company. Prior to taking that position he had served as the commander in chief of NATO forces in Europe. I paid him a visit at his hotel suite when he came down to Washington to confer with Reagan about the new appointment. This was before his Senate confirmation. I asked him to do everything he could to further improve Japan-U.S. relations.

Homma We are all familiar with Ambassador Mansfield's statement that "Japan-U.S. relations are, to the United States, the most important bilateral relationship, bar none," a position that he has reiterated more than once. By the same token, however, Japan-U.S. relations have always been crucial to Japan.

Official level Japan-U.S. relations have been cordial for a long time now. The United States has served us with numerous requests and even demands in the area of defense, but, in the broader context, the mutual trust based on the Japan-U.S. Security Treaty has, at the official level, continued to prevail. And at the level of everyday economics and popular culture, Americans are buying Japanese cars despite the trade deficit, are eating Japanese food in increasing numbers, and are beginning to express serious interest in Japanese culture in the broader sense.

In the wider context, there are these feelings of mutual trust on both sides, together with an awareness of the importance of Japan-U.S. relations. There is the deepening realization that our respective cultures are each fascinating in their own right and worthy of serious attention. And yet, paralleling these welcome trends, there is the deepening rift that is being opened up between us by economic and trade frictions. In the economic realm, our relations are tense.

Economic friction is not, of course, a recent phenomenon. We have been plagued by it, in one form or another, since the 1960s. However, as Japan's trade surplus with the United States grows, and as the U.S. fiscal deficit increases, the rhetoric in America becomes more shrill, and we wind up seeing these book titles like *Trade Wars,* and *The Japanese Conspiracy.* The irony in all of this is that it is an index of how close Japan-U.S. relations have become. Ambassador, you were right there in the thick of all this. It must have been pretty challenging at times.

Okawara When I first went to Washington in the diplomatic service, in the early sixties, I heard a lot about the *communication gap* and the *attention gap.* When I went the second time, in the early 1970s, it was the *information gap* that was seen to be at the root of all problems between Japan and the United States.

Thinking back on it now, I believe these gaps were partly responsible for the 1963 interest equalization tax shock during the Kennedy administration and the two so-called Nixon shocks in 1971, but it is also true that the Americans realized their mistakes in those cases, and determined not to repeat them. They took deliberate steps to eliminate the attention gap and the communication gap, and subsequently demonstrated a much improved understanding of Japan's importance.

What surprised me most upon arriving in Washington in 1980 was the tremendous breadth of the issues on which Japan and the United States were holding substantive dialogue. The breadth and substantiality of these ongoing exchanges would have been unthinkable in the 1960s. I felt very keenly that, in that sense, the communication gap had been greatly narrowed.

On the issue of the information gap, the number of American resident journalists in Japan has risen sharply. In the mid-1970s, if I remember correctly, the number of such U.S. reporters working in Tokyo was around 43. Now there are 79. Japan has 47 journalists assigned to Washington, including those in television. Japan also has journalists assigned to such major news centers as New York, Los Angeles, and San Francisco, so the total number of Japanese journalists in America is of course higher. If we compare only the corresponding numbers in Tokyo and Washington, however, the American journalists represent the larger force. There has also been a dramatic increase in the number of news stories filed in Tokyo. The quality of such reporting has sharply improved too. It can now be safely said that a day does not go by without the word "Japan" appearing prominently in every major American newspaper.

Homma That would have been unthinkable twenty, or even ten years ago, wouldn't it?

Okawara At one time, Japanese news stories were pretty much limited to earthquakes, typhoons, and other natural calamities.

Homma One might even have been able to write a single essay enumerating the instances in which "Japan" made it into the American newspapers.

Okawara Yes, but that has all changed now. The information gap has gotten much narrower, as well as the communication gap. Our two governments now regularly confer with each other almost on a day-to-day basis. Our elected legislators and our scholars exchange visits and information. Our respective business and finance leaders have far more contact today. One would think that our problems are also disappearing, but of course that is not the case. I am increasingly persuaded that it is the *perception gap* that now makes it necessary to exercise such caution in handling Japan-U.S. relations.

Americans can be quite stubborn. Once they come to a definite position on an issue, they are very reluctant to change their minds, much less have them changed.

There are fundamental contradictions between the way Americans view Japan and Japanese economic activity, and the way we Japanese view our own country and its activities. Therein lies the root cause of much of our bilateral friction. This seems to me, as I think back over the past ten or twenty years, to be an enormous problem.

Homma If a lack of communication is causing all the friction, the situation is not all that serious. All you have to do is open up more channels and increase the flow of communication, creating more opportunities for personal contact and mutual information exchange.

If instead, however, we are faced with this perception gap you have alluded to, Ambassador, the problem becomes a matter of fundamental perspectives and thought categories. This gets us into areas of ingrained notions, value systems, customs, and subconscious psychological factors. Now we can say that our communication is good, that our information is correct — so far so good. But the cutural framework within which we analyze and interpret that information is not readily susceptible to change. The problem is broader, of course, than the way the Americans perceive the Japanese. It involves the way Americans perceive Europeans, people from the Middle East, and Asians, and the way we Japanese perceive Americans, Europeans, and other foreigners. As we look deeper into this problem, we find ourselves in the realms of psychology and cultural anthropology. We are faced with something that we cannot change. We have taken a step up the ladder of progress, only to find that the situation is far more serious than we had previously supposed.

Okawara In terms of our economic relations, we experienced the "dollar blouse" problem in the mid-1950s, and then the textile wars in the late-1960s and early-1970s. I think these were symbolic developments in the history of Japan-U.S. economic competition. Then we began to export color TV sets, steel, motorcycles, and a lot of other merchandise. This gradually gave rise to a feeling among U.S. industrialists that they were being terribly victimized in their competition with Japan. The height of this sentiment was reached, I suppose, in the big problem over automobile exports to the United States. This product-specific trade friction then gave way to problems involving fundamental competition between Japanese and U.S. companies. I think that is at the root of Japan-U.S. friction today. The Americans think they are being seriously hurt in this competition, and that if things continue the way they are now, the problem will become extremely serious. The Japanese do not believe they are hurting the United States all that much. Japanese goods being imported into the United States are of extremely good quality, and the quality of life of the American consumer is rising accordingly. Certain U.S. companies may have something to complain about, but Americans in general are benefiting enormously. That is the Japanese perspective, as revealed by the results of a survey made recently by a newspaper company.[1]

---

1. On May 15 and 16, 1985, Asahi Shimbunsha [publisher of a major Japanese daily newspaper] conducted a nationwide survey on the subject of Japan-U.S. trade friction. Some of the results were as follows:
   - One person out of two said that radical measures should be taken to eliminate Japan's enormous trade surplus.
   - Sixty percent of those surveyed said they were deeply offended by Japan being singled out as the villain by foreign countries.

From the standpoint of employment and company management, however, there is a growing perception among Americans that the biggest problem is Japanese competition. While the United States was taking so long to recover from the second oil shock, the Japanese were investing in plants and equipment, pushing ahead with automation in every phase of industrial production, and thereby changing the entire base on which their competitive power rested. That is the American perspective. The Japanese are not conscious of the fact that anything like that happened. They do not believe they have seriously hurt their American competitors. They ask what is wrong with responding to a preexistent demand for quality Japanese goods. This is one extreme example of the perception gap.

Homma What kind of situation must we have in order for the United States to be satisfied? Japan has gone far in opening up its markets. Her import duties are much lower than those exacted in Europe. If American officials say we have to lower them further, then we might do so, and eliminate all of the remaining import restrictions. If the Japanese surplus still persists after that, we can say with confidence that it is the result of fair competition, based on our more efficient economy. Is that where we are headed?

Perhaps the Americans are saying "Look, we know that achieving balanced trade is not merely a bilateral affair, but if you Japanese open your markets and engage in economic

---

- Those surveyed were nearly evenly divided on the issue of future export policy. Some (38%) advocated a policy of restraint, taking the receiving country's situation into account and limiting exports if necessary. Others (39%) advocated abandoning restraint, seeing nothing wrong with exporting as much as possible to acquire foreign currency.
- Public opinion was also divided on the issues of imports and free trade. Some (46%) were in favor of restrictions in order to protect domestic industries. Others (42%) advocated an open-market policy.
- Only 12 percent of those surveyed said they would cooperate with Prime Minister Nakasone's appeal for each person to buy $100 worth of foreign goods.
(Asahi Shimbun, morning edition, May 27, 1985)

activity that is fair, according to our definition, then your surplus will shrink by itself. If that surplus doesn't decrease, then Japan must be doing something that isn't fair." Is that what they are saying? Will they keep demanding more "fairness" until the surplus disappears?

Or maybe they are saying something like this: "We recognize that Japan is trying to open its markets. We understand all the economic arguments in terms of pure economics. But your surplus in the Japan-U.S. trade is really far too large. Measures based on theoretical economics are not enough. You're going to have to make some political decisions and reduce your surplus. If you don't, then the free trade system that the Reagan Republican administration has championed so resolutely is going to crumble. By hook or by crook, you've got to bring the surplus down." Is that what they are saying?

There are several possibilities here. What, Ambassador, is your understanding of the matter?

Okawara I think the gut feeling of those in U.S. industry is that they want to eliminate competition with Japan. In other words, there is a deeply rooted notion that American companies are losing their viability because they can no longer adequately compete against foreign industry in general, but especially against the Japanese. And when that notion gets linked directly to government policy, the result is import restrictions. If such measures do eliminate the competition with Japan and other foreign trading nations, the troubled companies are satisfied. That's the corporate perspective. There is also the consumer perspective. And there is also the point of view that import restrictions are inconsistent — in the long run — with the fundamental American economic policy of holding down inflation.

Homma And in the long run, that's not the way to develop international competitiveness.

Okawara We are familiar with the proposal of import surcharge, by means of which domestic industries hope to suppress foreign imports. In the short run, this policy may give troubled industries a shot in the arm. In the longer run, however, it does nothing whatever to strengthen such industries. The consumer feels the impact of this in terms of higher prices for imported goods. His or her livelihood suffers accordingly. This policy also fuels inflation in the U.S. economy. For these

169

reasons the Reagan administration has taken a stand against such policies.

Economically speaking, the import surcharge is a clearly counterproductive policy. And yet it rears its head in Congress year after year. The reason is simple. Industrial interests with influence in Congress keep hoping to eliminate foreign competition.

The Reagan administration has consistently articulated its position on this issue. The import surcharge is a bad idea. The free-trade system must not be allowed to crumble. And there are some in Congress who keep arguing the same position, but they seem recently to be increasingly convinced that there is nothing more they can do to stem the rising tide of protectionism.

I believe that Japan should go all out in opening its markets, and thereby encourage those beleaguered free-trade advocates in Congress to take up the challenge again, with renewed vigor and determination. If the Japanese are not going to give to American products the same competitive opportunities that we give them, argue the neoprotectionists, then we must slap them with import surcharges and demand import restrictions in the name of reciprocity. That is why I urge that Japan will resolutely open its markets. I think this is the most important and urgent task now facing us.

Homma There are various domestic problems that make it difficult to go all the way in opening up Japan's markets. If that were not so, much more progress would have been made by now. It is a very difficult thing for the government and the ruling Liberal Democratic Party to go through with, but it absolutely has to be done. Unfortunately, however, even that is not going to immediately resolve the trade friction and surplus problem that plague Japan-U.S. economic relations. I think we must also look for other things that can be done to improve those relations.

Okawara I must confess that I too fear that the trade imbalance will persist no matter what Japan does to open its markets and promote imports. Be that as it may, however, the crucial task for us now, I believe, is to remove all possible grounds for the charge that Japan is playing unfairly, or that the Japanese market excludes outsiders.

In my opinion, Japan will not have taken adequate measures

To resolve Japan-U.S. economic friction so long as there remains any ground for the charge of unfairness.

Whenever the unfairness charge is leveled at Japan, it is commonly accompanied by the following line of argumentation: For Japanese businesses, the Japanese market and the U.S. market are absolutely the same. Japanese companies don't have to concern themselves about the Japanese market being this way, or the U.S. market being that way. When American companies try to move into the Japanese market, however, they quickly run up against things that don't exist in the U.S. marketplace. That's the problem. That's why it's unfair. Trade should be a two-way street, with imports allowed to move as freely as exports. But Japan tries to make it a one-way street, promoting exports and discouraging imports. That is the argument. We have to be prepared to persuasively counter this argument.

Homma During your five years in Washington, Ambassador, you must have heard those words *fair* and *unfair* used excessively. Those words do not always mean the same things to Americans and Japanese, however. Are there any criteria for resolving the differences? Who judges the winner here? My point is that there is a problem when the stronger opponent says "follow my rules and things will be o.k." You can end up with each side bolstering its own ego, saying whatever it likes. Then the Japanese will say "this is the way we operate our economy; what's wrong with it?" And the United States will say "this is the way the American economy has always functioned, in conformity with the noble principles of free trade." When the confrontation reaches this stage, who is to arbitrate?

One approach is, I suppose, to make adjustments based on the standard of economic rationality. Or you can emphasize how significant the free-trade system is to Japan, to America, and to the world, and how this concept is more or less embraced and agreed on by both parties. This gives you a kind of consensus, within the scope of which both sides can operate freely.

As a matter of stated principle, of course, both the U.S. and Japanese governments consistently extol the virtues of free trade. Japan's economy, however, traces its postwar recovery from the black markets in her bombed-out cities and through the so-called Korean War boom. During those early years of reconstruction and development, there were areas that benefited greatly from American assistance. Japan's economy, of course, owes its current prowess primarily to the vitality and resourcefulness of the Japanese people. Nevertheless, it is undeniable that Japan's success in creating the environment for this prosperity was contributed very significantly by America's vigorous leadership — leadership which has prompted historians to speak of "America's century" and the "Pax Americana." Much of this story tends to be forgotten today, but it behooves us to reflect upon it from time to time. America, however, has lost much of its formerly overwhelming power to influence global affairs. The Reagan administration is doing its best to restore that power. In the meantime, however, Japan has become an extremely powerful competitor in the international marketplace. When we look at this economic development, though, and ask ourselves whether there has been a commensurate recognition by Japan of its growing responsibilities to cooperate in maintaining the free-trade system, the answer seems to be "no." There is a sense in which Japanese industrialists are happy to reap all the benefits of free trade. They reason that it is perfectly natural for the outflow of Japanese products to keep swelling, so long as the market and the demand are there. The doctrine of free trade benefits most the economic entity that is the strongest. Well, there's nothing inherently wrong with being the most favored beneficiary, but it takes something more than that to achieve meaningful relationships in the international community. I feel that our vision is too dominated by pure economic theory.

Okawara Yes, one gets into difficulties if he tries to explain everything purely in terms of economic theory. I think that we Japanese are prone to fall into this error. As you have reminded us, Professor, our postwar economy has benefited from American aid, support, and cooperation in achieving its present prosperity. In currently popular Japanese economic thought, however, there is little place for a forthright recognition of that historical fact. At the same time, while outsiders see Japan as a mighty economic power, we Japanese do not see things that way. If it is true that Americans and foreigners in general tend to overestimate Japan's economic strength, it is no less true that we Japanese tend to underestimate that strength. We look at our everyday way of life and find it difficult to see ourselves as all that powerful. With most of us living in such cramped living quarters, maybe we will never shed this overly modest self-appraisal. Ironically, however, there is some tendency among us recently to think that Japan is superior in everything, and to view everyone else as inferior. Look at our phenomenal productivity, our massive exports, our great competitiveness, we say. And we brush off America now as almost insignificant. At least that's the way we come across to Americans. So, we disparage ourselves on the one hand and boast of our prowess on the other. Recent Japanese behavior seems to be marked by this strange contradiction.

Homma Perhaps a large part of that contradiction is a generational phenomenon. Those Japanese above a certain age still remember the hard times, and their appraisal of Japan's economic power tends to fall far below that of the international community. They think in terms of the limitations on Japan's strength. Some of those below a certain age, however, betray an attitude of overconfidence, which often looks to Americans like sheer arrogance. What is common to both of these generations, however, is a failure to recognize the current extent of Japan's international influence. In my view, Japan's international influence has now become a major factor in today's world — in the economic sphere, in the defense of the free world, and in the realm of culture. And yet the very Japanese who wield this influence are not fully aware that they are doing so. I think that describes the present situation.

Okawara I think that is precisely what is at the root of all the arguments in America about "fairness" and "unfairness." Take for example the case of the resolution which the U.S. Senate adopted on June 20, 1985, calling for Japan to bolster its defense capabilities.[2] In some circles in Japan it was argued that this

2. On June 20, coinciding with the visit to America of Defense Agency Director General Koichi Kato, the U.S. Senate passed, by a vote of 77 to 7, the Supplemental Appropriations Bill which included an amendment that called for Japan to strengthen its defense capabilities. This revision contained four main provisions, as follows: (1) Ja-

resolution was tantamount to a blatant demand by a foreign power which constituted meddling in Japan's internal affairs. In American eyes, however, Japan was simply not pulling its own weight in fulfilling its rightful international obligations. This was apparent in defense matters, it was felt, but even more conspicuous in economic matters. I think we may understand this as the underlying rationale for the American charges of "dirty pool" and "unfairness."

Homma What worries me in that regard, Ambassador, is the possibility that, as Japan has become a more powerful international presence, many Japanese have lost their former interest in world affairs. In other words, we may have lost something of our former perspective of internationalism. Following the war, Japan experienced several years of occupation, during which it was completely isolated from the international community. Then the Peace Treaty was signed in San Francisco, and gradually, in one field after another, Japan's international status was restored. During these critical years, those in positions of leadership and influence in Japan were fired with an urgent desire to discover what must be done in order for Japan to endure, to coexist, and to prosper in the international community of nations. Today, whether we like it or not, Japan's influence in the world is growing larger and larger. In spite of that fact, however, I'm afraid that we may have somehow compromised our former international sensitivity.

Maybe it is not very important, but linguists tell us that we Japanese now use an enormous number of English words in our everyday conversation. It has become fashionable for Japanese magazines to have English names instead of Japanese names. These names are not merely written in Japanese *kana*

---

pan should reconsider the defense guidelines adopted in 1976. (2) Japan should prepare a 1984 medium-term planning estimate that by 1990 would provide protection of sea lanes out to a distance of 1000 nautical miles. (3) Japan should increase its appropriation for U.S. military installations in Japan, as well as increase its share in defraying labor costs within the framework of the Status of Forces Agreement. (4) The United States Government should report to Congress by February the following year concerning Japanese defense efforts.

characters or Japanese *romaji*. They are English words written with English spelling. One might think that this phenomenon reflects a love for English—the international language—or a desire to sharpen international sensitivities. Actually, it is quite the reverse. English words are finding their way into everyday Japanese at a rapid rate, but this merely represents a process of converting English vocabulary to Japanese vocabulary. It is an inward-looking phenomenon. Interest in looking outside has in fact weakened.

It is now fashionable for new couples to go abroad for their honeymoons. Hakone and Miyazaki used to be the popular spots. Modern couples prefer Guam, Fiji, or New Zealand. This trend, however, may have nothing at all to do with any heightened interest in international matters.

We are becoming an increasingly major world power. But this development is not being paralleled by a proportional growth in our recognition of either our rightful share of international economic responsibilities or our proper role in maintaining the security of East Asia. There are, unfortunately, a number of reasons for this.

In the final analysis, we Japanese have rebuilt our nation—following our defeat in the Pacific War—under a new constitution that was created during the American occupation. This historical fact may be partly responsible for the situation I have just outlined, but, even so, we ought to have developed a stronger sense of responsibility. If such a sense does not develop to any substantial degree, then we expose ourselves to the dangers of jumping into nationalism, ultranationalism, and jingoism. I wish I could say that at present no warning signs are to be seen, but I hesitate to say I could and that worries me.

Okawara I am kind of like Urashima Taro or Rip Van Winkle, returning to Japan after serving nine years in Australia and America. I am amazed by the proliferation of foreign words and phrases today in our everyday life. Not only are they liberally scattered through our conversations, but everywhere we look we see signs and advertisements covered with *romaji* and English. I seriously doubt whether there is another country in the world that is this inundated with foreign words. But, as you suggested earlier, it does not seem to reflect any heightened international sensitivity on the part of the Japanese people. One begins to think that using a foreign language and developing international sensitivities have nothing whatever to do with each other.

175

We used to hear a lot about Japan's insular mentality. To be sure, Japan is a small country. In a former era we Japanese were interested only in narrowly preserving our insular ways, and had no international influence whatsoever. Then came the great national transformation. We entered the modern era, and now wield tremendous international influence, both economically and politically. Our mentality, however, has not been adequately transformed. We continue to think of ourselves as a little island kingdom. Our behavior is not consistent with what and who we are. That is where the problem lies.

Indeed, there is now operative a kind of reverse insular mentality in which we are oblivious to any embarrassment that our behavior may cause our foreign friends. I think we see this mentality clearly in the economic realm. And I think it is a major reason why we are now being censured not only by the United States, but by the European nations and our Asian neighbors as well. God help us if we let a narrow-minded jingoism get the upper hand in our society. In no previous era has it been so pervasively crucial for us to behave as citizens of the international community, to make our vision a truly global one, and to hold to ideas that make sense internationally.

Until we Japanese develop such an international mentality, we will continue to have problems with the United States and other countries, frictions will multiply, and we even expose ourselves to the risk of becoming an international orphan.

Homma The United States is a nation of immigrants, and in one sense its entire history is marked by an open-door, open-armed policy toward the peoples of the world. This is in stark contrast to Japan. By the same token, however, people flocked to the United States from all over the world to become Americans. They initially created a rather strongly centripetal or inwardly-focused society and for a long time were not very interested in what went on abroad.

I allude here, of course, to America's traditional isolationism. Until World War II, the United States was not a nation that embraced deep international sensitivities.

This was a nation where people lived in places like Kansas City, where you could stand and gaze at the horizon in any direction, where there is nothing but land as far as the eye can see. People were born, lived, and died without ever seeing the ocean. It is no mystery why early America did not develop great international sensitivity. Following World War II, however, in a great irony of history, the burden of safeguarding international order was thrust upon this traditionally isolationist nation. Americans became keenly interested in world problems, and their government became active in international diplomacy. The United States became, as it were, the custodian of postwar history.

Turning to other areas, Ambassador, you traveled extensively throughout the United States during the five years you were assigned to Washington. Tell us something of your impressions of and experiences in the various states.

Okawara It took me four and a half years to get around to all fifty states, making speeches wherever I went. You mentioned Kansas City, Professor. The Midwest was indeed once a bastion of American isolationism. Now the same region has developed a strong international consciousness due to its farm produce exports. Indeed, it is the midwestern states that have most staunchly supported free trade. This fact points up the danger of trying to use outdated information in one's endeavor to correctly understand the United States.

We often hear about the economic center of gravity shifting from the North and Northeast to the South and Southwest, or that the population is shifting from East to West. The sunbelt region is now said to be the center of U.S. industrial activity, and I did in fact find that a lot was going on there. We also hear that the demographic center of gravity has shifted from St. Louis to Kansas City, and that California has now become the largest voting block in the United States. This does not mean, however, that New England and the Great Lakes region have fallen on hard economic times. The entire economy has become much more decentralized, it is true, and there is an ongoing transition now from the old smokestack industries to new high-tech industries. A lot of high-tech industry is in fact springing up in New England, as I saw for myself when I went there.

Another thing I found, wherever I visited, was a very strong interest in Japan. Many state governors now believe that promoting closer economic ties with Japan is the best way to insure the economic development of their respective states. As a consequence, some governors have personally led economic missions to Japan. Twenty-seven states now maintain liaison offices in Japan. The task of attracting Japanese business to these states is taken very seriously. Nowhere is that fact better reflected than in the strong trend now underway in the state legislatures to abolish the unitary tax (which has posed the biggest obstacle to foreign investment in many states), even to the point of fiscal sacrifice. It might behoove us to pay even closer attention to this trend.

As is frequently remarked, Washington, D.C., alone does not represent America, and one has to see the whole country to understand it. It is also often said that one must know what grassroots Americans are thinking, and what their hopes and dreams are, in order to understand the real America. After traveling throughout the United States, I think I can fully endorse that statement on the basis of my own personal experience.

Homma "America watching" has entered a particularly important phase, and is in fact more difficult than before. The United States used to be one national entity, a noun that could take a singular verb as it were. And I'm not going to argue here that America is not a single unity. It is important to recognize that it is one nation, with one president, under one federal legislature.

However, as you just pointed out, Ambassador, there have been many changes in the fifty states. Farmers in the formerly isolationist Midwest, for example, are now very sensitive to international developments. With such widespread changes now in progress, we Japanese need to take a more serious approach in our watching of America, gathering information on America, analyzing America, and understanding America.

As I read our Japanese daily newspapers and magazines, I continually encounter these hastily concocted theories on America. You know, such and such happened in America today, therefore America will become this way or that tomorrow. But if you read this material again a year later, you find that the writers never really understood what was going on in America.

I think that it is increasingly necessary for us to continually bear in mind two major facets of America, namely the vigorous, dynamic side of American life, and the fundamental American spirit that has prevailed since the nation was founded.

Okawara As was first pointed out long ago, Japanese journalists

178

in the United States are concentrated in Washington and New York, so naturally their news is slanted toward the Washington-New York perspective. This situation evidently still prevails today, although more and more reporters are venturing into regional America, and writing interesting stories for us. Journalists lead very busy lives, and it is difficult for most of them to get away from Washington and New York. If they are given more opportunities to go into regional areas, however, a more comprehensive view of America will begin to reach Japanese readers.

There is a story about a news conference held in Washington in March 1985, by Tokyo Electric Power Company chairman Gaishi Hiraiwa. The story gives us an anecdote on American diversity. Hiraiwa was leading a survey team of public relations activities on a tour through the United States at the time. "In Los Angeles, I was given friendly heartfelt suggestions," said Hiraiwa. "In New York, I was given sound and judicious advice. In Washington, I was given a warning accompanied by scathing criticism of Japan."

Some go so far as to say that the farther you distance yourself from Washington, the more apt you are to understand American feelings and circumstances. I suppose that is a paradoxical recognition of the peculiar atmosphere which hangs over Washington — a city of politicians, lobbyists, and lawyers. Even so, if you want news, Washington is the place to be.

Homma We're talking here about what it really means to "understand" America, aren't we? Take the Japanese fellow that gets invited to the home of an American who lives in Los Angeles, is crazy about Japan, and has the interior of his home done in mock-Japanese style. The guest claps his hands and says "Gosh, Americans really are pro-Japanese!" Though it might be true of *that particular* American, the generalization is false; the guest has failed to understand America. It is very true that New York and Washington are not America, but America nonetheless does contain New York and Washington. I think we have to continually balance our receptivities and sensibilities between these two paradoxical perspectives.

Okawara It is very dangerous to base generalizations about America on a brief acquaintance with, say, Los Angeles. Unless the foreign observer in America is unusually circumspect, he usually ends up emphasizing just one aspect of the country. In the case of us Japanese, this seems in some ways to be inevitable.

Homma But can anything be done to keep from falling into that trap? I suppose that efforts to avoid the common pitfalls must be redoubled in every field, whether government service, the media, academia, or whatever. But the problem really involves all Japanese people, doesn't it?

Okawara Well, if I may allude to something which I have seen at close hand, I strongly believe that for the purpose of the grassroot level contact we should promote more sister-city activities and sister-state relationships. If we could increase personal contacts and substantive exchanges at the city and prefecture/state level, it would help us enormously to understand one another as human beings. In these exchanges between diverse cultures, there is a direct experience of our mutual human commonality that cannot be acquired in the abstract. I think that a lot of our difficulties arise because we try to handle too many things solely through formal government-to-government channels.

As I have said many times concerning postwar Japan-U.S. relations up until recently, Americans have entertained a cold, brittle image of Japan, perennially associating Japan with automobiles, color TV sets, stereos, VCR's, cameras, and other hardware. Americans are particularly conscious of the automobile, which is so indispensable to their everyday lives. That is why the automobile readily becomes a target and a symbol for criticizing or denouncing Japan. And the cold, brittle image of Japan has exacerbated problems between the two nations.

Americans today, however, are beginning to bring softer, warmer things from Japan into their everyday lives, as witness the Japanese food boom, the sushi craze, the new interest in Japanese fashions, and the sumo competition held recently in Madison Square Garden. And with this new trend has come a corresponding change in the American image of Japan. That image is now beginning to include facets that are softer and warmer. This development is necessary and welcome. And to reinforce this more human image of Japan, there needs to be more person-to-person contact. If we can promote much more of the kind of social exchanges that grow out of such contacts as sister-city relationships, we can deepen personal ties between high school students, college students, and ordinary working citizens. I think that would be extremely meaningful.

Homma Whenever economic friction increases, as it recently has, talk of Japan-U.S. relations always turns quickly to economics. Economics is important, of course, and we naturally must give our full attention to it in such cases. But we have to go beyond this purely economic dialogue. We have to develop richer human relationships that are based on mutual cultural appreciation as well as reciprocal economic interest.

I read a recent column in the *New York Times* by James Reston in which he said that the most popular course at Harvard University is on economics. We all know how important economics is, but I think we tend to overemphasize it. I really think that our endeavors to solve economic problems go awry once our approach to them becomes purely economic.

Okawara Difficulties always arise when we try to make economics the rule for everything. We Japanese, in particular, tend to approach every issue with economic theory and economic rhetoric. This does not change opinions or solve problems. The problems between Japan and the United States, in particular, are beyond the help of mere rhetoric.

Homma Not that we should entirely eschew rhetoric per se. There is a place for rhetoric, of course, for openly setting forth the logic of one's positions. But that by itself is not enough.

By the way, Ambassador, I understand that while at Tokyo University you took Dr. Yasaka Takagi's course entitled "U.S. Constitutional Law, History, and Diplomacy." Those lectures were originally given as the Hepburn Lectures at the Imperial University Law Department. Dr. Takagi began delivering those lectures around 1924,** after studying in the United States, and continued them right through the Pacific War. Dr. Takagi passed away in April 1984. A collection of his papers entitled *In Search of The American Spirit [Amerika Seishin wo Motomete]* was published posthumously by Tokyo University Press and has now been followed by a second edition.

***

**Translator's Note: Yasaka Takagi first gave the Hepburn Lectures in 1918, before studying at Harvard.

This may seem trivial to some, but Dr. Takagi was a pioneer in scholarly research on the United States, and I think his story gives us reason to be encouraged about the future of Japan-U.S. relations. Some readers are no doubt of that generation that could have heard Dr. Takagi lecture, but I believe some of the younger readers will also be interested.

Just as we Japanese endeavor to understand the spirit of America, so likewise do Americans seek to comprehend the spirit of Japan. We need to put more substantive content into Japan-U.S. relations, so that the spirit and the feelings of our two nations are duly recognized and understood. Then when we meet to discuss our various responsibilities, we will be able to set forth and compare our respective positions, openly and nonconfrontationally. The relationship between our two great nations deserves the efforts that it will take to make it that good.

Okawara Unfortunately, I don't believe that Dr. Takagi's lectures were that widely understood when they were being given, which is particularly sad to me as one of his students. However, it is truly thrilling to know that now, forty or fifty years later, those lectures are getting another hearing, and are being enthusiastically received. This is a sign, I think, that the Japanese people do keenly sense just how important the United States is to Japan, and how much we need to understand that country in a proper perspective.

Despite all the things that are being said, the Japanese man and woman in the street realize that they must take Japan-U.S. relations very seriously. And I think they are deeply concerned about the current state of those relations.